The
MASTERS' Secrets
of
BOWHUNTING
DEER

by John E. Phillips

Book 3 in the Deer Hunting Library
by Larsen's Outdoor Publishing

ISBN 0-936513-34-9

Library of Congress 93-78226

Published by:

LARSEN'S OUTDOOR PUBLISHING
2640 Elizabeth Place
Lakeland, FL 33813

PRINTED IN THE UNITED STATES OF AMERICA

4 5 6 7 8 9 10

DEDICATION

A man's life is made up of his experiences, the people he has met, and the things he has done. Very few sportsmen become bowhunters without the help and assistance of others. Even primitive man passed down from generation to generation the archery skills and bowhunting tactics we use today. Bows were used for hunting and war 35,000 years ago. We all are debtors to those first archers.

This book is dedicated to the men and women who have given up their time to teach me the sport, to show me better ways to bowhunt and to introduce me to new tactics that have made bowhunting one of my favorite outdoor activities. Many of the people mentioned in these chapters have helped guide and instruct me through my continuing education in the sport of bowhunting. This book is dedicated to them.

ACKNOWLEDGMENTS

Very few writers work alone. Many hands are required to forge the words, bend the paragraphs, make the sentences fit, compile and edit the photos and make sure the page numbers and the art are in the right place. This book, like all the others I have done, have required the efforts of many dedicated people.

My wife, Denise, was the driving force who brought all the parts together. Sandi Hildreth's mastery of art as demonstrated on the cover and throughout the book in the unique drawings and illustrations helped bring my words to life. Ellery Cook spent hours researching material, typing chapters and putting in corrections. Marjolyn McLellan was the grande dame of our work force. Not only is she an excellent typist, but she is a super-good mother-in-law who works diligently to help complete the work. Mary Ann Armstrong, after working all day as a secretary, came in at night and helped with editing and typing. The masters of bowhunting whose knowledge and wisdom you read about in these pages gave of their time, skill and knowledge freely and without hesitation. Without these men and women, this information never would have reached these pages. I want to thank each one of them.

PREFACE

Knowing our history is an integral part in predicting our future. If we don't know where we have come from and who we are, we can't try to pre-predict where we are going. Modern archery, as we know it today, began in 1911 when Californians discovered an emaciated Indian who spoke no English, any known Indian language or even Spanish. An anthropologist took charge of him and named him Ishi. After much trial and error, anthropologists were finally able to communicate with Ishi by using a language known as Yona, the language of a tribe of Indians believed to have vanished.

Ishi was treated at the University of California Medical Center by Dr. Saxon Pope. From Ishi, Pope learned how to make bows and arrows and how to shoot them. Pope and his good friend, Art Young, began to hunt with Ishi. Later Pope and Young hunted all over the world with their bows and arrows and founded the Pope and Young Club, which keeps bowhunting records today.

Wooden bows were popular hunting weapons until the late 1940s. In the late 1930s, the static recurve bow was developed. In 1950, fiberglass began to be used to improve strength and durability. In the 1950s, bowmakers learned how to mass produce bows. Although the compound was first assembled in the late 1930s, the idea for the compound was not really developed until the late 1960s. Because the compound reduced the amount of weight an archer had to hold when he drew the bow, thousands of sportsmen, including women and children, began to take up the bow for sport.

Today there are more than 2-1/2-million bowhunters nationwide. And, the National Sporting Goods Association says, ''Archery is the fastest growing sport among women.'' Archers spend approximately $420 million per year on archery equipment and supplies, a major impact on the economy. Because most states now have a separate bowhunting season, many sportsmen have taken up the bow because they can increase the numbers of days they are permitted to hunt and the number of animals they can bag.

In this book, you will learn strategies and tips from some of the greatest bowhunters in the world. Each of the hunters mentioned in these pages not only knows the ways of the whitetail but also has an abiding love for the strong bow and the swift shaft.

Bowhunting allows me to find and get close to deer like the archers of old.

ABOUT THE AUTHOR

John E. Phillips learned to bowhunt the hard way. His first bow sight was a nail attached to his bow with a rubber band. On his first bow hunt, he shot 24 arrows at deer and never touched an animal. His first tree stand was homemade. Since he fell out of it three times in one day, he quickly abandoned the idea of becoming a tree stand manufacturer.

Phillips has spooked deer, missed deer and caused deer to stare at him in wonder and amazement as he has hung upside down while trying to get into his tree stand. However, after much trial and error, many bruises, scrapes, scratches, cuts and nicks, he finally has become a bowhunter and today takes deer each season with his bow.

Phillips wrote this book to prevent you from having to go through the pain, agony, disappointment and discouragement he did when he first took up the bow. He was not fortunate enough to have master archers teach him lessons in bowhunting like you will find in these pages. But later as he learned from the masters, he recorded their wisdom to better help you enjoy your sport.

For more than three decades, John E. Phillips has hunted whitetail deer. He even chose to attend Livingston University in deer-rich Southwest Alabama to be able to deer hunt daily during Alabama's liberal deer season, which runs 3-1/2-months each year. Phillips also has been a student of deer and deer hunting as an active outdoor writer and photographer for more than 20-years for both newspapers and magazines.

Phillips, the author of 13 other outdoor books, has had more than 1200 articles published on deer hunting. An active member of the Outdoor Writers Association of America, the Southeastern Outdoors Association, the Alabama Press Association, the Alabama Sportswriters' Association and Outdoors Photographic League, Phillips has won numerous awards for excellence in writing.

You never will see John Phillips in a tournament shoot or at an archery range. He is a woodsman who prefers the solitude of a tree stand overlooking a deer trail and the competition of bowman against buck. Phillips's philosophy of bowhunting and life in general is that he is the consummate student on a continuing quest for knowledge.

He says, ''I want to study and learn all I can about the outdoors until I have dirt thrown in my face when I am 6 feet under the ground. I hope my tombstone will read one day, 'He studied, he learned, and he left behind the wisdom he found for others in the outdoors.'''

CONTENTS

Dedication 3
Acknowledgements 4
Preface 5
About the Author 7

1   Master Bowhunter's Secrets For Success 11
2   Gear Up For Bowhunting 23
3   Choose Your Broadheads To Suit Your Style 35
4   Improve Your Arrow's Flight Accuracy 41
5   Are Tree Stands Friends Or Foes? 47
6   Avoid The Common Mistakes Bowhunters Make 55
7   Solve The Difficult Problems Of Bowhunting 63
8   Make It Happen In A Tree Stand 71
9   Hunt Your Buck Indian Style 81
10 Understand The Body Language of Deer 89
11 Use A Master's Secrets To Bag Bucks 97
12 Bowhunt The Bucks Of Gun Season 107
13 Know Nuts To Take Bucks 115
14 Women With Bows 123
15 Return Of The Longbow 133
16 A Trio Of Bow-Killed Trophies 141

Index   149
Resource Directory 151
About The Artist 160

CHAPTER 1

MASTER BOWHUNTER'S SECRETS FOR SUCCESS

The difference between an archer and a bowhunter is an archer shoots targets with a bow and arrow at a measured distance. For the archer to be successful, he simply must have a target in front of him and shoot accurately. But the bowhunter must be able to shoot accurately in many different positions after finding a place where a deer will present a shot within the effective range of his bow.

One of the best bowhunters I ever have met is Jerry Simmons of Jasper, Alabama. In 80 days of one season of bowhunting, Simmons let arrows fly at 53 deer. He harvested 43 of these whitetails.

One of the primary reasons for Simmons' success is because he finds places in the woods to put his tree stand where the deer will walk to within 18 yards or less. Simmons, who has over 30 years of experience, spends most of his time scouting. He has developed a system of scouting which has helped him to harvest more than 300 deer with a bow in his lifetime.

HOW TO BEGIN

Like most good bowhunters, Simmons appreciates having the advantage of maps as he says that, "Topo maps and aerial photos will show you where woods openings are in the forests. These maps will give you an idea of the terrain, show you where the creeks and valleys are and where the trails and roads are located on the property. I've found the most critical element in successful pre-scouting is knowing the road systems of the land you want to hunt.

"After I have an overview of the area from the maps, I next drive the roads. A hunter must identify the kinds of trees on a region to determine where he should start looking for a place to hunt. A bowhunter also must know what foods the deer prefer and where these foods grow during the early season, the middle of the season and the late season to scout effectively.

"If river bottom hardwoods are present on the land, you need to pinpoint what kind of acorns grow in that section of the woods. If an area

11

In many areas, deer seem to prefer acorns, probably because they haven't had any since winter.

has hills and mountains, you must learn what kinds of foods are on those ridges.

"For instance in my part of the country, the first acorns to fall usually are the mountain oak acorns. These trees are found on the tops of high ridges and mountains. When these acorns first start dropping, the deer feed on them heavily. As soon as the other acorns fall, the deer will quit using the mountain oak acorns. Perhaps the mountain oak acorns don't taste as good as the other acorns.

"When I scout, I try to find mountain oak trees on high ridges first so I can hunt them the first two weeks of bow season in my region. Then I search for the white oak or water oak acorns for the third week of hunting and on into the middle of the season.

"In my area, deer seem to prefer acorns -- probably because they haven't had any since the winter. The first acorns that fall concentrate and draw the deer. In my early season scouting, I'm looking for those trees that will drop their acorns first and concentrate the deer. To locate trees where acorns are falling at the first of the season, you need to know which trees release their acorns first.

"But the acorns are not the only food source I scout for at the first of the season. In the South, persimmons and crabapples also will draw deer, although this food source is short-lived. Deer can eat these fruits up in about a week. To be an effective scouter, you must know what the deer will eat when you're hunting and that that food source actually is providing the food during that time.

"Always remember the only way you can bag deer regularly is to take them when you know what they're doing. Of course, you can harvest a few deer accidentally. However, to be a consistent bowhunter, you must be able to take a deer when it is feeding, working a scrape or traveling a trail. You've got to understand what that animal is doing, besides when and where he is doing it. Scouting helps you more accurately predict where the deer are, what they are doing and when they are doing it.

"To scout and locate food trees, the hunter must be familiar with what the bark, leaves and fruits of various trees look like. If you understand what the leaf of the tree is, you can search for the leaf, find the tree, see whether or not the tree has acorns on it and if it has dropped any of them. Also by knowing the tree's leaf, if you find a leaf on the ground of one of the food trees you want to hunt, you'll know that tree is in the vicinity. Then you can start hunting for it. Or, if you can recognize a tree by its bark, you can identify a tree easier and quicker. By locating the fruit or the nut of a tree, you'll know exactly where to hunt. Although most sportsmen don't realize how important tree identification is, this knowledge drastically can reduce the amount of time you must scout."

WHAT ABOUT DROPPINGS?

The deer's droppings often can reveal what the deer is eating. In one particular place, Simmons found deer droppings to be the key ingredient to his successful scouting program.

"Most of the time you can't tell what a deer is feeding on from its droppings," Simmons explains. "But every now and then, the deer's droppings will provide a clue that can lead you right to their primary food source.

"Several years ago I was scouting under some acorn trees when I discovered some deer droppings. But these droppings were purple instead of the usual deep, chocolate color associated with deer. Immediately I knew the deer were feeding on purple poke berries, which is the fruit of the poke sallett plant found in many areas of the South.

"At first I didn't think too much about the droppings, because I assumed perhaps this individual deer had found a few poke berries somewhere and had eaten them on the way to the acorn tree. But as I continued to scout in different areas, I found quite a few purple droppings in varied locations. I decided the deer in this region were feeding heavily on poke berries and realized if I could find a poke berry patch I should be able to see deer.

13

"Then I remembered a 2-year-old clearcut was about 300 yards from where I found the purple droppings. I also knew poke sallett grew well in a clearcut. I headed for the clearcut. The closer I got to the clearcut, the more purple droppings I spotted. When I arrived at the clearcut, I found plenty of tracks, droppings and evidence the deer were eating the poke berries.

"I climbed a nearby tree. In a short time, I bagged a buck. Although droppings may not give you any information, studying them is worthwhile, because many times droppings may provide just the clue you need to locate and take a deer with your bow."

WHERE YOU SHOULD BE

Simmons not only scouts to determine where the deer will show up but also to find a tree he should be in when the animals do appear.

"Sometimes I worry myself nearly sick trying to decide which tree I should climb and put my tree stand in. But deciding which tree to place your stand in is time well-spent, because you must put it in a tree where the deer will pass within 18 yards or less. Let's look at three different options bowhunters may have for treestanding.

"The first option is the food tree itself. Although the tree dropping the food may appear to be the perfect tree to climb with plenty of cover in it, the right size for your tree stand and adequate back cover, when the deer approaches this particular tree, he always will come straight at you -- which is one of the worst shots a bowhunter can take. I have found the best time to bag a deer is as soon as he gives you the opportunity to shoot within range. If a deer is moving straight toward you, quite some time may pass before he turns sideways to you, which delays your shooting time. A deer walking towards you can see you better when you are straight in front of him.

"I wouldn't totally eliminate standing in a food tree, because there may not be another tree close enough to it in which to place my stand. But, if at all possible, I prefer to use a tree that doesn't offer as many advantages as the food tree in order to get a shot at the deer's side.

"Another tree within 15 yards of the food tree may have plenty of cover too. But perhaps from scouting, you learn the deer will be coming from behind you from a bedding area along the trail that passes under the tree to get to the food tree. Although you can turn your stand to face the deer as they come down the trail, once again you'll be trying to take a head-on shot, which I don't think is a good shot. The tree may be a skinny tree with not many limbs on it to break up your silhouette or may be in an open region that won't provide a good background to break up your silhouette.

"I've learned if I can have at least one limb below my tree stand, then I am less likely to be spotted by the deer. I believe when a deer sees a limb

14

Jerry Simmons learns where the deer are feeding to know the best spot to put up his tree stand.

at the base or on the trunk of the tree, then he believes everything from that limb up is safe. I also like to have leafy limbs around me. I use a small, portable, hand saw to trim limbs. Then I'll have holes to shoot through in the tree. But if this secondary tree doesn't have a limb below me and is relatively clean, then probably I will eliminate hunting from this tree.

"The perfect tree for a stand is a tree off to one side of the food tree. If from the signs the deer seem to be approaching from right angles to that tree, then you will have a broadside shot. I'll choose a tree that either has numerous limbs I can hide in or a big trunk so that my silhouette will be broken up against the tree. I prefer to place my stand in a large-trunked tree, because I have to worry less about back cover. Too, I believe the deer are less likely to see me.

"The type of tree stand I use allows me to adjust my stand to fit any size of tree in the woods. I search for a tree with vines growing up the sides of it, which also aids in breaking up my silhouette and hiding me better. I want the deer to come in to that tree at less than 18 yards. Then I believe I have a better than average chance of bagging the deer."

Simmons also categorizes his hunting areas as "morning places," "middle-of-the-day spots" and "afternoon areas." He scouts to determine exactly what time a deer will show up in the regions they are using.

This system of scouting can be compared to a pattern within a pattern for the bass fisherman. For instance, an angler may locate bass on hardwood trees that have fallen into the water. But the bass only may be at that place at daylight, at dark or in the middle of the day. To successfully catch the bass, the sportsman must fish during the hours the bass are on the structure.

The same is true of deer hunting. Just finding a region deer are using is not enough information to accurately predict when deer will show up. Many hours can be wasted in a tree stand waiting on a deer that may not appear until after dark. Here's the types of areas and the times of day Simmons believes are the most likely to produce deer.

The Morning Place

According to Simmons, "A morning place usually will be close to a bedding area and also may be a good afternoon place. To identify a morning place, I look for a food source relatively close to a bedding area. Most of the time, a deer will come in to bed down and eat just a bite or two before he goes into that bedding region.

"A prime example of a morning place is the spot I found this past hunting season. A farmer had left many soybeans in the middle of his field and the deer were going into the field at night and feeding on the soybeans. No beans were left around the edges. Then the deer would leave the field before daylight. The woods around the field were a mature forest with no understory, making the woods a relatively open region the deer had to continue through before they reached their bedding site, which was about a half a mile away where the property had been clear cut.

"Since I knew deer didn't like to get caught in the open during daylight hours, I took a stand about 300-yards away from the bedding area along the trail the deer were using. I could count on the deer to show up from daylight until 7:00 a.m. I never saw a deer in this area past 7:00 a.m., but I took five whitetails there. This spot was definitely a morning place."

Middle-of-the-Day Spot

"The middle of the day is a good time to bag deer, and I've taken quite a few deer in the middle of the day," Simmons recalls. "The kind of place I look for to hunt at this time is a thicket with some type of food tree in the middle of it or on the edge of it.

"For instance, a white oak tree, which is a good food tree for deer in my section of the country, with numerous limbs to shade out the ground may be a good choice. If I can set up close to that white oak tree, I can harvest a buck with my bow when he comes in to feed.

"During the middle of the day if the deer are being pressured, they generally will remain in a thicket. But they will not lay down all day in that thicket. They will stand up and move around, get something to eat and lay down again. Since five or six deer may be holding in a very small thicket, various deer will move, eat and lay back down at different times. This is not to say that deer won't come out into openings during the middle of the day because they will. However, I have discovered I consistently bag more deer in the middle of the day hunting close to a food source in or near a thicket."

Afternoon Area

"In the afternoon, deer are more than likely to be moving toward fields and openings to feed after dark," Simmons mentions. "Although many bowhunters will set up on the edges of fields to hunt in the afternoon, if you can locate a food source close to the field, your chances are better of taking a deer than if you set up on a field. If you know deer are feeding in a soybean field at night, but you also have found a swamp chestnut that is dropping its acorns about 175 yards from the soybean field, then set up near the swamp chestnut tree to try and take the deer coming to the field. More than likely, the deer will move in and feed on the swamp chestnuts for a time before dark and then walk on to the field.

"Although you may think this region is a morning place, it's not. Since the deer are already full from feeding on the soybeans all night long, in the morning they will walk past that swamp chestnut tree without eating when they are heading toward their bedding area before daylight.

"When I'm scouting, I attempt to determine not only where the deer are feeding and what they are feeding on but when they are eating. Then I can maximize my hunting time in the area and at the time of day when I am most likely to have a shot at a deer."

Other Productive Regions

Bottlenecks

"I believe the very best place to take a deer is where the habitat is squeezed down to a very small neck of woods like a bottleneck," Simmons reports. "These spots generally will be good all season and for many years -- as long as the habitat doesn't change drastically. The ideal bottleneck contains food on one end of the neck and a bedding area on the other end. If I only hunt one type of region for deer, this area will be my choice. Once you've located this kind of place, you don't have to continually scout.

Saddles

"Saddles in mountains are very good sites to consistently harvest deer. I define a saddle as a low spot in mountainous country where the deer easily can walk through mountains without having to climb the mountains. The easiest way to discover these types of areas is with a topo map. Many times the outline of a saddle will jump out at the hunter on a topo map but will have been difficult to find in any other way.

"I located two saddles like this in my home state of Alabama that consistently produced deer for several years. These saddles were areas deer used to travel from one region to another. I learned then that as long as the habitat didn't change much, saddles regularly would pay deer dividends year after year.

Patch Browse And Fruit Trees

"Patch browse, which in my part of the country during different times of the year may include poke sallett, smilax (greenbriar) and Japanese honeysuckle, often can be a very dependable deer attractor. Fruit trees too can be a productive area to hunt in the early part of the season in the South. If you are fortunate enough to be able to hunt around an orchard, the trees are easy to find. But if you are hunting in the woods, the deer most often prefer crabapple and persimmon trees in my region. I specifically look for these fruit trees when I am scouting.

Scrapes

"Every bowhunter knows that hunting over scrapes produces deer. I usually set up within 18 yards and downwind of a scrape. If the buck is coming in to work the scrape, you must be close enough to take him with a bow. But you always want to make sure that you are downwind of the scrape and broadside of the deer when he moves in.

Escape Routes

"Once deer have been pressured, especially by gun hunters, then they will flee from that hunting pressure using escape routes. Late in the season, I hunt escape routes that either lead into or out of thick cover. To hunt these trails effectively, the bowman has to know what time the hunting pressure begins in this region, how far the deer will have to travel on these trails, and what time he must get into his stand to bag the deer during daylight hours.

Thickets

"Also thicket hunting can be extremely productive -- if the sportsman understands what the deer are doing in the thicket. Deer not only hide and bed in a thicket but also feed. Most thickets have plenty of deer food in them and may even hold the deer's preferred food. Deer also travel through thickets to move from one place to another rather than walking through open woods.

"Often I will begin to scout for deer in heavy cover, because there's more than one reason for a deer to be there. I try to put my tree stand inside a thicket rather than hunting on the outside. More often than not, you will see more deer in the heavy cover than on the outside of it.

"Although I realize there is no such thing as a surefire place where

Setting up his tree stand in the most productive tree is critical to Simmons' bowhunting success.

you always can find deer, I thought I had such a spot when I hunted a saddle in the mountains of North Alabama. For four years in a row, that one location produced deer for me very season. But then the area was clear cut, grew up in a large amount of thick undergrowth and became so thick I couldn't hunt it.

"I'm convinced even today that this area would have remained a productive bowhunting spot forever -- if the land use hadn't changed. But when the land use was altered, I had to look for a new region to hunt. Good hunting areas don't last indefinitely. However, any of these places will be productive spots to bag deer during certain times of the year and under particular conditions. But none of these regions will always produce deer all during the year forever. That's the reason the sport is called bowhunting and not deer shooting. The bowman constantly must be scouting for a place to hunt."

WHEN TO HUNT WHERE

According to Simmons, "The first thing I do every morning of hunting season is to turn on my weather radio to find out the wind's direction. Even though I may have 20 places in the woods to hunt, the wind direction often will eliminate all but a few. I won't go to a stand site if the wind will carry my scent into my hunting area, or if once I am in my stand, the wind will carry my scent in the direction from where I think the deer will be coming.

"Although the weather radio gives me my first basic information about wind direction, I don't rely solely on it. In the woods, I check the wind direction with my compass to determine where I'm going to hunt.

"Another factor that enters strongly into my decision on where I will hunt is the terrain of the area where I am hoping to take a stand. Oftentimes hills, valleys and cross-currents actually can change the wind direction in a region. To hunt effectively, you've got to understand how the terrain affects wind direction. I believe the wind tells the sportsman where he can and can't hunt. No matter how many deer I think I may see in a particular spot, if the wind is wrong, I don't hunt that region.

"The second factor I consider is how much time has elapsed since I've hunted a particular spot in the woods. If I've seen deer in a place the day before, not returning to that same area the next day is difficult. However, I believe in letting a region rest from hunting pressure.

"I usually won't hunt from the same stand two consecutive days. Sometimes the wind won't permit me to hunt from the same stand two days in a row. If I have anywhere else to hunt on the second day, then I won't hunt from the same stand I did on the first day. However, I may return to that particular stand in two or three days, if the wind is favorable, because deer generally will not remain in a specific spot for very long. If you allow an area to rest too long, the deer may be gone.

"Another ingredient to be considered is whether you spend your hunting time around a food tree or a food plot. If you intensively hunt for several days and either take or spook deer around their food supply, they simply will locate another place to eat."

THE IMPORTANCE OF FOOD SUCCESSION

To harvest as many deer as Simmons has over the last 30 years, he has had to know the food succession deer follow. Deer are browsers and will eat a variety of different things. However, they do have their preferred foods. Often when a bowhunter can find the deer's favorite food in short supply and high demand, he can concentrate deer to within the effective range of his bow. Although most hunters know this information, some fail

20

to realize the food deer have been feeding on the week they scouted may not be the same food deer will be eating the week they plan to hunt. "In my area, deer like to feed on muscadine vines," Simmons comments. "If you go into the woods three weeks before the season and discover a bunch of muscadines, you have found a good place for deer. "But when you return later, the muscadines will be gone, and so will the deer. I have learned that the muscadine supply will be depleted when hunting season arrives. But deer often will feed on poke sallett, crabapples, persimmons and mountain oak acorns during the early season in the South.

"If you hunt the same area for several years, you will learn that most of the time the trees that drop their acorns first one year also will release their acorns first the following year. I am talking about individual trees of the same variety. For instance, there may be one mountain oak tree in the high country that is the first tree to drop its acorns, which will concentrate the deer under that tree. Once I discover which particular tree releases its nuts first, I'll return to that same tree in the early part of the season the second year. I've found the same to be true of most varieties of oak trees over which I hunt. Also the trees that hold their nuts the longest usually will do so each year and make better late season hunting regions.

"Yet another trick I've used to find deer food in the wintertime is to follow the redwinged blackbirds, which live all across the U.S. These birds migrate into our area in the late deer season, peck acorns open and eat the meat. They also knock many acorns off the trees.

"Once I was hunting near some flooded timber and heard numbers of acorns hitting the water. I went to where I heard the noise and observed blackbirds eating acorns and knocking them into the water. Since then I follow the blackbirds, which often will lead me to the food trees that are still holding their acorns late in the season. After the blackbirds knock the acorns to the ground, the deer can feed on them. Agricultural crops too are good sources of deer food, even after they've been harvested, because usually some of the crop is left on the ground for the deer to eat.

"Oftentimes a bowhunter can change locations and increase his odds of bagging deer when there is an abundance of food for the deer to eat. For example, one of the deer's preferred foods is the white oak acorn. If you can locate one or two individual white oaks dropping their acorns, the deer will concentrate there, and you can harvest them. But if numerous white oak trees in the region you're hunting are all releasing their acorns, the deer will be scattered, making the hunting much harder.

"One of the ways I took more deer last season when the acorns in my area had all begun to drop was to hunt in another part of the state where

21

the white oaks were fewer and had just started to release their nuts. The white oak acorns concentrated the deer. In the late season, I also look for foods like greenbriar, Japanese honeysuckle and maybe a few trees that are still dropping nuts in my region.''

HOW TO SCOUT FOR SPOOKED DEER

Late in the season, hunters have trained deer to utilize trails and different terrain breaks. The best places to hunt at this time of year are saddles in mountains and funnels.

"You don't learn how to scout for spooked deer the first day you go into the woods,'' Simmons explains. "During the year, you will begin to notice trails that lead away from regions of high hunting pressure. One of the best places to hunt is a bottleneck where the terrain is restricted by two different types of habitat coming together and necking down the woods or necking down the thick cover. Where a clearcut and a field come close together and hardwoods are on either end is a good example.

"Another productive area if you're hunting in the mountains is to find a saddle where the deer can cross without having to climb the mountain when hunting pressure builds up on one side of the mountain. Of course the deer look for the easiest escape routes. Where the terrain is restricted, a hunter often can find good trails to hunt deer that are trying to escape hunting pressure.

"I've been hunting deer for over 30 years, and I still learn something each and every time I go into the woods. I don't learn as much now as I did when I first started hunting, mainly because there is only so much you can know about deer and hunting. I've devoted thousands of hours to understanding deer, deer habitat and what influences deer.

"Something I'm starting to understand is that the whole sport is a jigsaw puzzle. Although each piece is critical to solving the puzzle, how the pieces fit together and what bits of information you can add to other information you've gathered is the most important aspect of deer hunting.

"The successful bowhunter must know deer behavior and what and when a deer wants to feed on as well as the effects of hunting pressure. He must:

- work hard when he is scouting,
- scout from daylight to dark,
- practice patience in a tree stand,
- learn to shoot accurately from all kinds of positions and through all types of cover,
- spend thousands of hours bowhunting and
- have a burning love for the sport to consistently be successful in bowhunting for deer.''

CHAPTER 2

GEAR UP FOR BOWHUNTING

Since the days of Robin Hood and William Tell, hundreds of years have passed, millions of deer have been hunted, and thousands of hours have been invested in bowhunting technology. Archers today may feel a kinship to a particular kind of bow that's been developed through the years, with their equipment reflecting their bowhunting heritage. The bowhunter is not simply a hunter but is a stylist who matches his bow to his preferred type of hunting, to his philosophies and beliefs of what bowhunting should be and to what he feels is the best way for him to personally take an animal. Bowhunting has become so diversified a sport that today the archer has many different options as to the kind and style of bow he'll select, and the way he'll hunt.

What kind of bow is best for you, and what type of hunting will satisfy you the most? Clarence Yates, who has taken more than 100 deer with a bow in his home state of Alabama, has been a bowhunter for most of his life. The proprietor of Yates' Archery Shop in Birmingham is an expert at outfitting new bowhunters. He discusses several types of bows and bowhunting equipment as well as their advantages and disadvantages, the style of hunting they represent and the kind of archer who chooses them.

THE BOW

"When a sportsman walks in off the street and tells me he wants to become a bowhunter, I first look at his physical appearance," Yates says. "If the customer is short, I wouldn't want to recommend a long bow, because it may inhibit his ability to shoot. If he is very tall, he will be pulling a much longer draw. Then I want to help him pick out a bow that will give him the added draw length. The outdoorsman of average size can use almost any bow on the market.

"I also try to determine strength by physical appearance, but sometimes this is deceiving. Just because a man is big doesn't necessarily mean he's strong. A short man may have a lot of upper body strength. But the hunter's height and strength often give me the clues as to the type of bow I will recommend for bowhunting."

23

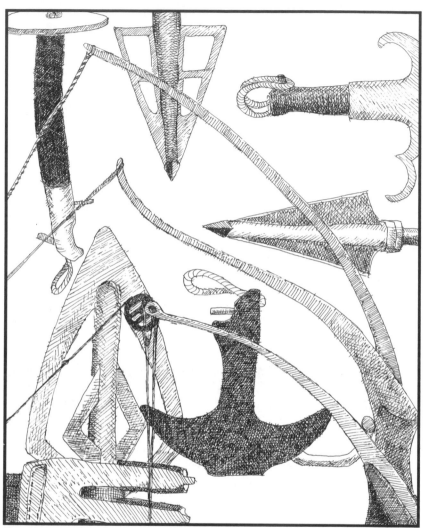

Bowhunting has become so diversified a sport that today's archer has many different options on the kind and style of bow he selects and the way he hunts.

The Longbow

Is the longbow a dinosaur in today's Space Age? Does it really have a place in the world of compounds, overdraws and arrows that fly faster than 300-feet per second? The answer is definitely yes.

Don't forget that some of the greatest archery shots ever made were performed with the longbow by Howard Hill of Vincent, Alabama. With his longbow, Hill took many of each species of North America big game and also many African big game animals. He was also the first white man to ever down an elephant with a bow and arrow. Because Hill took a charging lioness with his longbow and shot an apple off a man's head, we know the longbow in the hands of a master shooter can be very accurate and deadly. But the longbow may be difficult to learn to shoot.

I asked Clarence Yates, who has shot and hunted with all kinds of bows, to describe the type of hunter who will prefer the longbow and to name some of its advantages and disadvantages.

"The longbow hunter usually falls into one of three categories," Yates explains. "Either he started shooting a longbow and never changed, he shot a recurve bow for awhile and decided to try a longbow, or he shot a compound for several years and wanted to shoot a bow that was more challenging and traditional.

"The longbow hunter believes he's accomplished more than if he bags that same deer with a compound or an overdraw. Shooting a longbow captures some of the romance of the sport; the bowman hunting with a longbow has taken a deer like the Indians once did. He also calls to mind the men who dressed in Lincoln green and hunted in Sherwood Forest. The tradition and history of hunting with a bow are captured when the archer takes a longbow into the forest.

"Some other advantages have made longbows popular. Longbows are rugged. You can beat one on the side of a tree and still go out and shoot it successfully. With no moving parts, longbows are also quiet. Also when shooting a longbow, all you have to keep from losing is the string, the bow and the arrow -- and not a lot of other equipment and accessories.

"The biggest disadvantage of using a longbow is because it's so long, it can be hard to maneuver if you're hunting in close places. Too, the limbs may touch something and will keep you from aiming properly. If you're kneeling to shoot, you may have to drastically cant the bow to get off a shot, keeping in mind that a 64-inch length is considered a short longbow. A longbow is also not as easy to shoot as a compound. More strength is required to pull it back to full draw. However, the longbow will throw a heavier arrow straighter and further than a compound will.

"Don't sell the longbow short. Longbows have taken numbers of deer. They still bag many deer every year, and I'm sure they'll take plenty of deer in the future."

The Recurve

The recurve bow was actually the first improvement in bows in thousands of years.

"The recurve is somewhat smoother to draw than the longbow, and it's shorter, averaging about 60 inches in length," Yates reports. "The arrows for these bows, especially aluminum arrows, shoot faster than the arrows for the longbow."

Since longbow shooters are traditionalists, they usually choose wooden arrows, whereas recurve bowhunters are beginning to become more modern and often prefer aluminum shaft arrows. Yates shot a recurve for eight years and took 26 deer with it.

"The advantage of the recurve over the longbow is the little curve over the tip of the bow, which acts as one more catapult to throw the arrow faster than a longbow can," Yates comments. "Since recurves are longer than the average compound, a 60-pound recurve takes a fairly strong shooter to draw and release it. A novice bowhunter once asked me when does the recurve break-down, referring to the let-off a bowhunter experiences when he's shooting a compound. I told him, 'As soon as you turn loose of the arrow.'"

The basic disadvantage of both the longbow and the recurve is the hunter must draw the bow and release the arrow as soon as he's at full draw. The sportsman doesn't have the advantage of holding the shot like he does with a compound. Most longbow and recurve archers are instinctive shooters out of necessity. Shooting either of these two bows is completely different from shooting a compound, since both require the archer to be able to pull and hold more weight than the compounds do. However, both the longbow and recurve are considered more traditional than the compound, which some purists believe is a product of the Space Age and a perversion of the sport.

"The bowman who chooses the recurve is probably someone who started out shooting a recurve before the compound bow ever came to the market," Yates mentions. "Because this bow has been his first love, he never has seen a need to change after he has become proficient with it.

"Recurve shooters like the feel of that kind of bow. Each type of bow has a certain feel to it. When an archer finds the feel he likes, he'll usually stay with that kind of bow, often for the rest of his life.

"Another reason an archer will choose a recurve is because he has confidence in it. The recurve bowhunter probably has taken deer with his recurve and has become very proficient with it. He's developed the philosophy that his style of hunting allows him to bag as many, if not more, deer than his counterparts who are shooting compounds. In other words, what's not broken doesn't need to be fixed.

"Also no bow is better for shooting fish than a recurve, because the archer can shoot quickly and accurately. Getting a shot off at a fish you

Choosing the right bow is critical to your bowhunting success.

only see for an instant is often the difference between taking and not taking a fish. Moreover, if the hunter faces a charging wild boar or a bear, he wants to be able to draw and shoot as fast as possible. If you draw the compound quickly, you may throw the arrow off the rest, and you may have to take a little time to aim before you shoot. But the recurve draws smoothly, quickly and can be released instantly.

"I quit using a recurve and began to hunt with a compound, because the compound shot more easily and with greater speed. Although I can shoot a 60-pound compound with ease, shooting a 60-pound recurve strains me. Also the compound gives me some extra time to refine my aim, since I can hold the compound longer at full draw than I can a recurve."

The Compound

"The compound definitely shoots the arrow faster than a longbow or a recurve," Yates observes. "The bowhunter can shoot a 70-pound compound with much more ease than he can a 55- or 60-pound recurve or longbow. A compound may be somewhat more difficult to draw until it breaks over, but once the bow lets-off, it can be held easily. Even though the bowman is holding less weight when he's at full draw with a compound, once he releases the string, the energy returns into the bow. Then the bowman picks up the maximum weight of the bow to throw the arrow. Another advantage of the compound is the trajectory of the arrow will be much flatter than either with the recurve or the longbow.

"I was a traditional archer who held out for several years before changing to a compound. However, when I was shooting tournament archery with my hunting friends, I noticed my arrows rainbowed into the target, whereas arrows from their compound bows seemed to skim across the top of the ground and go straight into the target without dropping. When we went to the target to pull out our arrows, I realized their arrows were deeper in the target than mine were, which indicated to me that their bows were producing much more force than my recurve bow was. I had to face the fact that this compound bow I had resisted for so long was, in fact, superior to my recurve.

"The typical modern archer shoots a compound. More than likely, he never has drawn either a longbow or a recurve. Often the modern archer is a two-season hunter, who hunts with a bow during bow season and a gun during gun season. When he goes into a store today, he observes that 90 to 95 percent of the bows being advertised and displayed are compounds, and only 5 to 10 percent of the merchandise will be longbows or recurves. Because of the sheer numbers of compound bows he sees, the modern hunter most likely will select one unless he's hung up on tradition.

"The compound also has allowed a larger segment of the outdoor population to enter the archery market. The compounds are easier to draw, easier to aim with the new sighting systems available, are shorter and easier to carry, and enable a beginner to reach a level of proficiency much more quickly than longbows or recurves."

The Overdraw

The latest ripple in the new wave of archery is the overdraw, which allows the archer to draw the tip of his arrow back further than the front of his bow. Because it facilitates shorter, and thus lighter, arrows, overdraws are able to throw an arrow faster than a normal compound bow, with some approaching 300-feet per second. But as of right now, Yates is not an enthusiast of the overdraw.

"Personally, I like the longer and heavier shaft the compound shoots," Yates says. "I also prefer the heavier broadhead I can shoot with my compound, but may not be able to shoot with an overdraw. However, the advantage of the overdraw is that it shoots arrows very fast. It gives arrows a very flat trajectory.

"When overdraws first came out, I didn't think as much of them as a hunting weapon as I do now. I didn't believe the lighter arrow would penetrate as well as it does. The overdraw pushes the arrow at such a high velocity that, even though the shaft is light, it has great penetration. I don't believe we'll ever see the day when overdraws will replace the compound. But the day is fast arriving when probably 50 percent of hunters will be shooting them. Right now, I think that overdraws account for 25 to 30 percent of the archery market.''

I asked Yates if he was concerned that the more modern bows may be perverting the sport of archery, as some bowmen feel.

"Yes, I am," he replies. "Some of the newer bows are being made with such a dramatic let-off that they're not even like bows to me. The Safari Club and some state departments of conservation have agreed that a 65 percent let-off will be all they will recognize for bowhunting. I'm afraid that if there aren't some standards imposed, we'll have bows that cock themselves like a gun, and I don't think that's what bowhunting is all about.''

Bowhunting is a very individual pastime, and the type of bow a hunter chooses is as personal as the kind of underwear he selects. Each bow can be mastered with a high degree of accuracy. Choosing between them largely depends upon how you perceive bowhunting as a sport and how steeped you are in tradition.

How To Choose A Bow

According to Yates, "If a beginning hunter is of average stature and strength, I think several bows will be best for him. Generally speaking, I will not recommend the more expensive bows for a beginner but rather the medium-priced ones. Since all of these bows effectively will take deer, before a hunter spends a lot of money on equipment, I want him to be sure he will enjoy bowhunting. If he does fall in love with the sport and determines he wants a more expensive bow, by that time he'll have enough experience in hunting and shooting to know exactly which bow he prefers. I usually offer new archers a choice of several, average-priced bows as well as a more expensive bow and the least expensive one I have.

"Generally, there's not much difference in how bows shoot, regardless of how they're priced. The price of the bow is more often determined by the cosmetics of the bow and the extra gadgets put on it, rather than not how well it shoots. A sportsman often may spend a lot of money on his first bow and not have any better bow to learn on than if he had bought a far less expensive one.''

DRAW LENGTH AND PULL

"After my customer decides which bow he's most interested in, I next check his draw length and the weight of the bow he most comfortably can pull," Yates says. "Draw length is the most important factor in choosing the right bow for the hunter.

"To determine the hunter's draw length, I have him pull several different bows with various draw lengths. I have the archer draw the bow and make sure he can pull the bow all the way back and anchor his shot on the corner of his mouth. This positions the string just beside the eye to help him aim and shoot better. If he can't comfortably bring the string back to the corner of his mouth and hold it there, then most likely the draw length is too short. If he pulls the string back, and it comes past the corner of his mouth at full draw, the draw length is too long.

"Draw length determines arrow length. Once I decide on the sportsman's draw length, I choose an arrow that protrudes at least 1/2- to 1-inch past the front of the bow, to make sure he'll have adequate broadhead clearance. Then the bowhunter won't accidentally bump the broadhead on the front of the bow -- even if he gets excited and attempts to pull the bow further than it's supposed to be drawn.

"To check for proper draw weight, I have the customer pull bows of different weights to determine what he can pull without having to strain or be uncomfortable. Choosing a draw weight that can be held comfortably and then increasing the weight as the novice becomes stronger is much better than having him fighting a bow too heavy for him to draw. A beginner must understand he doesn't need to shoot with the heaviest draw weight he possibly can pull, because the strain will cause him to shoot inaccurately. The average hunter initially should be able to pull about a 55-pound compound. Once he becomes stronger, he then should be able to pull 60 to 65 pounds comfortably."

THE QUIVER

"Because loosely-carried arrows are dangerous -- even if they don't have broadheads on them -- I recommend that all beginners buy quivers," Yates advises. "Most hunters favor the types of quivers that bolt onto the sides of their bows and can be taken off their bows easily once they get into their tree stands. Some quivers twist and lock on the bow, others have quivers that can be taken on and off with small knobs."

THE ARROW

As Yates further explains, "Once I determine the arrow length a bowhunter needs and the poundage he will be pulling, we then can refer to a chart provided by the arrow companies to see what spine most appropriately matches the draw length and the weight of the bow he plans to shoot. (Spine refers to the stiffness of the arrow.) The archer usually will have several types of arrows to choose from that will be spined to fit his draw length and weight.

"Normally I suggest the beginner purchase six arrows, probably the least expensive grade of arrow. After he's practiced with these arrows, he then can decide if he wants to buy more expensive arrows for his bow."

THE BROADHEAD

"The beginner doesn't need to think about broadheads when he's just learning how to shoot a bow," Yates comments. "However, some

To be able to successfully arrow a deer, you must have the correct equipment.

sportsmen want to buy all their bowhunting equipment at one time. There are so many broadheads from which to choose the beginner can get frustrated and confused trying to decide what he needs. The main thing I stress for a beginner, if he's going to be shooting a 55-pound bow or less, is that he not buy a broadhead that weighs more than 125 grains.

"The broadheads I suggest are the Bear Grizzly, which is an inexpensive, four-blade broadhead, or the more expensive Thunderhead 125 or Satellite Titan stainless steel 125, which I particularly like because it has a bladed head. It cuts from the very tip of the point through the length of the broadhead. Another productive broadhead is the Rocky Mountain three-bladed broadhead called the Ultra. For the hunter shooting a heavier bow, I recommend the Razorback 4 & 5, which are 140-grain broadheads."

THE RELEASE

"Unless a beginner has made up his mind he wants to shoot with a mechanical release, I don't suggest using one," Yates mentions. "But a tab is good for novice bowhunters. A tab is easy to use and fits on the second finger of the shooting hand. It's tight enough so that it stays in place, making it harder to lose than when using a mechanical release.''

THE FOREARM GUARD

''About one-third of the people who shoot archery have to have an arm guard,'' Yates reports. ''The other two-thirds don't require arm guards because their arms are naturally slightly bent when holding a bow. Although two-thirds of archers won't need arm guards, I recommend the beginner use one. If the bow string is released and hits the arm, the string can cause a bad bruise. More than likely the beginner will be thinking about that string hitting his arm more than concentrating on the target. Since some shooting problems can be created that may require years to correct, until the novice can determine whether or not he needs an arm guard, he should start off wearing one. Interestingly enough, 98 percent of the women who shoot archery require an arm guard, because for some reason their arms seem to be straighter than a man's.''

TARGETS

''Most people want some type of target to practice shooting,'' Yates says. ''Although my shop sells expensive targets that can stop and hold broadheads or field points, I suggest the beginner buy a bale of hay or an paper target. Most novices want to start with a deer target; however, I recommend they choose a paper bull's-eye target. Having a well-defined spot at which to aim helps them learn more quickly how to hit that spot than if they choose a deer target and start off looking at the whole animal. Paper targets and a bale or two of hay are also the least expensive targets you can buy.''

SIGHTS

''About half of the people who buy bows today are putting some type of sight on them,'' Yates explains. ''For the beginner, I like the Cobra 4 pinsight, which can be adjusted horizontally and vertically. The best way to sight these pins is to begin with the top pin and shoot it at the target.

''There is a very simple rule of thumb to follow when sighting in with pinsights. Start off at 15 yards. If you miss the target, then move the pin toward the direction the arrow flew. For example, if the arrow hits low and to the right, move the pin down and over to the right. Once you have the first pin sighted in, set the second pin straight under the first pin, and you should have your left and right adjustments correct then simply adjust for elevation. The further you back up from the target, the more you lower the second pin.''

CLOTHING

''Pants probably are one of the most overlooked parts of the bowhunter's equipment,'' Yates advises. ''Although the six-pocket pants

The author believes that utilizing the correct gear is one of the major keys to success when bowhunting.

have caught on with gun hunters, I don't believe they're as good for the bowhunter as pants with four pockets. When stuffed full of hunting gear, side pockets often will get in the way of your bow when you're walking or when you're in your stand preparing for the shot. If you need more than four pockets, wear a backpack instead.

"The same is true for shirts and jackets. Pockets are nice, but they get in the bowhunter's way. I prefer relatively tight-fitting shirts and pants with few pockets. No matter what type jacket or pants you wear, try to eliminate buttons, which are noisy and can catch your bowstring.

"Choosing the right hat is extremely important to the bowhunter. There's nothing worse than pulling the string of your bow and having it touch or knock your hat off because the bill is too long. If you don't have a short-billed cap, use a hat with no bill or wear the hat backwards when you're ready to shoot.

"For all the gear we've discussed, a bowhunter can get into the sport inexpensively. At my shop, I give my customers instructions when they buy the equipment and ask them to come back after they've been shooting for a week. Then I can see how they're shooting and help correct any problems they may have developed.

"The novice bowhunter should choose his tackle from an archery dealer who will spend the time not only to match the tackle to the hunter but also to teach him how to use the gear he's bought. A reputable dealer can help the beginner with any problems he may have, and he'll enjoy the sport of bowhunting much more than if he tries to order equipment out of a catalog or walk into a store and buy what he thinks he needs without sound, professional advice."

CHAPTER 3

CHOOSE YOUR BROADHEADS TO SUIT YOUR STYLE

Selecting the best broadhead for you is not an easy task with so many claims made by each company. But to test a wide range of broadheads and to discover what qualities are most desired in them, Dr. Robert Sheppard, an independent researcher and bowhunting instructor from Carrollton, Alabama, recently compared the efficiency of more than 50- broadhead designs.

MATERIALS AND METHODS

In years past, broadheads were often categorized by general types such as "cutting edge" or "bullet point" designs. Today, however, most bullet-point broadheads have a cutting-edge-type appearance. Because of this trend, Sheppard made no attempt to categorize the broadheads.

Some of the heads Sheppard tested would not be legal in certain hunting areas because of their design or weight characteristics. For example, to be legal in Alabama, a broadhead cannot be barbed or weigh less than 100 grains. (Refer to game laws in the area you intend to hunt.)

For the test, Sheppard chose a Browning Mirage bow with a 29-inch draw and an adjusted 60-pound draw weight, which was a reasonable average. Shots were taken from 17 yards, since most whitetails are bagged between a distance of 12 and 20 yards.

After purchasing sides of beef, Sheppard shot arrows to test the heads' ability to penetrate tissue and bone. To maintain consistency, the same arrow weight and type were used throughout the test. A TM Hunter rest was utilized, and arrow-flight characteristics were kept as stable as possible through tuning techniques and adjustments of rests, nocks and tillers. To ensure the release pattern would not adversely affect arrow flight -- the most critical factor -- a Fletch Hunter mechanical release was used.

Blade thickness and head diameters were confirmed through the use of a machinist's caliper. Most measurements were very close to manufacturers' specs.

With ratings ranging from 1 (poor) to 10 (excellent), the broadheads were evaluated in each of the four following ways:

1) To determine broadhead penetration and hole characteristics, each head was shot five times into muscle. Then the heads were rated based upon the size holes they cut, plus the degree of penetration.

2) To gauge penetration in a consistent medium, each broadhead was shot five times into plastic foam and then rated based upon the degree of penetration.

3) To determine the broadheads' ability to withstand resistance upon impact, each point was shot five times into bone. The heads were then rated based on how well they penetrated without curling their points, breaking or bending their blades or disconnecting from their inserts.

4) Each broadhead was shot five times into 5/8-inch furniture-grade plywood to estimate how well each point could withstand passing through a dense medium having a more consistent texture than bone. Following that test, each broadhead was rated based upon how well it penetrated the plywood without bending, ripping off or detaching from the ferrule or mandrel.

RESULTS

After informally testing more than 50 broadheads made by 21 companies, here's what Sheppard found:

In general, the heads with various types of inserts did not seem to penetrate well when they encountered the dense materials of bone and wood. However, the Wasp High Tech, Muzzy's Matador and New Archery Products' Thunderhead were notable exceptions.

Sheppard also found another generality. "The wider and more numerous a broadhead's blades, the poorer it penetrated, however the greater the size hole it cut," Sheppard explained. "A surprising exception to this precept was the old standby Razorbak by New Archery Products, which penetrated well and cut holes larger than its 0.790-inch cutting diameter would suggest. This head was deadly despite the fact that it did not fare well upon encountering bone.

"I achieved similar results with Razorbak's cousin, the Thunderhead, also from New Archery Products. But the Thunderhead withstood contact with bone and wood mediums better than the Razorbak did."

According to Sheppard, another notable exception to the hole-slicing rule was Jeff Anderson's Magnum series of broadheads. These heads created holes noticeably larger than their cutting diameters measure, which is something Sheppard could not explain. However, the Magnum did not penetrate well -- most likely because of its relatively short length and wide blade angle. The smaller 363 and 243 Magnums penetrated

The single most important characteristic of a broadhead is that it fly straight from the bow to the target spot.

much better than the more popular 245 Magnum, unless it was used by a hunter who could handle an 85-pound bow in a hunting situation.

Sheppard discovered yet another broadhead characteristic. ''Long-bodied heads tended to penetrate deeply and stay intact upon encountering bone and wood. I never had noticed this trait before. Those broadheads measuring 3-inches long and 1-inch wide seemed to penetrate and withstand impact better than the 2-inch-long, 1-inch-wide or the 3- by 1-1/4-inch points.''

Passing the wood and bone tests commendably were Jerry Simmons' original Interceptor, as well as Simmons' newer, lighter version, the Land Shark; Delta's Nubbin; Satellite's Titan and Satellite's II; Zwickey's Black Diamond; and the Bear Razorhead.

''Simmons' heads had the thickest blades of any I tested and predictably held up when the going got tough,'' Sheppard reported. ''Also the concave design of the Interceptor caused it to enter hide better when shot from an extreme angle, which was a potentially helpful characteristic for a bowhunter who couldn't take a perfect shot.''

Other close contenders in the area of being nearly indestructible included: Roger Rothaar's Snuffer; Muzzy's Matador; Delta's Sniper and Nubbin; Satellite's Titan and Satellite II; Zwickey's Black Diamond; and the Bear Razorhead.

The bottom line was that numerous top performing broadheads are available to choose from, regardless of which set of performance characteristics you like.

CONCLUSIONS

What can we learn from these findings about broadhead penetration? Does penetration into a consistent medium like plastic foam parallel penetration into tissue?

Maybe.

Does a broadhead's ability to remain intact upon quick contact with bone mean it will kill quicker?

Maybe not.

Although the data from this study do show some general performance characteristics of broadheads, no further conclusions can be drawn from this exercise. The ratings are guesstimates; they're not scientifically achieved.

Scientifically testing the validity of even a single performance characteristic of a broadhead would be a difficult task as would be obtaining statistical information about a broadhead's ability to drop a whitetail of a specific size and weight within 25 seconds. To establish some pattern of consistency, a person would need to shoot approximately 100 deer from exactly the same distance, the same body angle and the same tree stand height while using the same bow, release, fletch, arrow spine, arrow weight, arrow diameter, string material, stabilizer, tiller adjustment, string silencer, draw length, draw weight, etc. Only under these circumstances could a small margin of error ever be achieved.

But even with all these factors being equal in standardized tests, variables would exist, including:
- The age of the animal (are older deer tougher?);
- The sex of the deer (are bucks tougher than does?);
- The relative humidity at the time the shot was taken (even a puff-type string silencer can slow arrow speed by more than 10-feet per second);
- The emotional state of the deer (was the deer relaxed or tense when the shot was made?).

As Sheppard mentioned, "Of the many whitetails I've struck, I doubt any two of them were shot from the same angle and at the same point of impact. Yet, like most serious hunters, I've drawn my own conclusions about bow, arrow and broadhead performance. My thoughts will likely surprise, if not infuriate you.

"I believe any bow from 40- to 100-pound draw weight is adequate for taking whitetails. I also think any arrow, regardless of spine, length,

Broadhead selection is more of a personal preference as proved by Dr. Robert Sheppard's test.

weight, diameter, fletch or nock, is just fine for hunting deer -- if it flies straight. I'm convinced that practically any modern broadhead will kill deer, if the point can be made to fly true.

"The single most important characteristic of a broadhead, in my opinion, is that it fly straight from the bow to the target spot. Any performance beyond this is fluff and does not necessarily add killing power. A broadhead the size of a hatchet blade flying at Mach 6 just over a deer's back is of no value to a hunter."

BROADHEAD TEST RESULTS

"The Bear Polar and Bruin should prove popular, but my test suggests that Fred Bear did it right the first time with the Razorhead. The four-blade model is the Polar; the 2- blader is the Razorhead.

"The Interceptor from Jerry Simmons was one of the best performers in all categories. Despite its weight, the Interceptor flew quite well from a light bow/arrow combination."

The Satellite performed well, which didn't surprise Sheppard since he's put many of these broadheads through deer.

The Black Diamond series from Zwickey was an excellent performer but lacked a screw insert.

The huge Snuffer from Roger Rothhaar was well-designed and indestructibly built, if you could pull enough poundage to make it fly.

Kolpin's Twister, with its somewhat slanted (not spiraled) blades, matched the performance of most other insert-blade heads.

Martin's Hornet, like many heads with insert blades, tended to shear its blades when encountering heavy resistance.

Although the Black Hole from Hoyt penetrated very well, its blades seemed to detach easily.

Anderson's 243 Magnum performed better than the larger and wider 245 Magnum, which did not penetrate as well.

Darton's Litening scored well for an insert-designed broadhead.

The 85-grain Chuck-It from Hoyt is deadly but illegal in some states because it is both barbed and weighs less than the required 100 grains.

New Archery Products' Razorbak 5 is a consistent performer in the field, even though it did not get high marks in the wood and bone tests. A 10-grain version could be one of the finest broadheads ever made.

The bullet-point design of the Rocky Mountain series from Barrie including the Supreme, the Razor, the Ultra, the Power Point and the Fast Flite, seemed to retard penetration, though these have proved effective in the field.

The Zapper from Bohning should be a good field head despite its difficulty with bone.

Delta's Nubbin is a super head that scored well in all categories. But the Nubbin has the disadvantage of lacking an insert. It must be sharpened before use.

The X-Cellerator from Browning should prove highly effective in the field.

The Bow Bullet from Hoyt was well-designed but lost just a few points because its leading point tended to curl upon bone and wood contact. In the field, however, the Bow Bullet should be deadly.

Although the Savora series of heads had a unique locking design, its blades tended to shear when passing through bone and wood.

The Blazer Max from Bohning was a good performer, but overdraw shooters might find its heavy weight difficult to tune.

The solid blades and chisel-type nose of Golden Key's Spinner seemed to hinder penetration, but the broadhead performed well upon meeting tough resistance.

The Matador from Muzzy scored better than most insert-type heads. Its replaceable practice blades would allow bowmen to practice with essentially the same head with which they hunted.

CHAPTER 4

IMPROVE YOUR ARROW FLIGHT'S ACCURACY
With Noel Feather

Bowhunting is an exact sport. To shoot accurately, your equipment must be in the very best shape it can be. I always make an equipment check the day before I hunt; I never assume my equipment is in the same condition as it was the last time I hunted.

I make sure that all the nocks on my arrows are securely glued to the shafts and that no cracks are in them. If a nock is loose or cracked and either slips or breaks when it's released, you'll miss the deer. Check the nocking point on your bowstring, too, to see it hasn't slipped or moved. Also look at your sight, and notice if it has been jarred the last time you've hunted or loosened during the trip home in the car. If your sight is not tight and in the proper position, you can't make an accurate shot. Also, don't overlook your peep sight if you're using one. If the peep slips, is not tied in properly or becomes loose, your point of impact will change. You won't hit where you aim.

One important piece of equipment often overlooked is the arrow rest. If the rest moves or slips, then the broadhead can't fly straight and true. Another factor that makes a big difference in your bowhunting ability is determining whether your broadhead and your shaft are in line with each other. If the broadhead and the shaft aren't in line, then the arrow will not fly straight. To test your broadhead, stand the broadhead on its tip and spin the arrow like you would spin a top on a piece of glass or a countertop. A broadhead that doesn't wobble is in line with the shaft.

The best way to insure accurate shooting is to eliminate problems before you shoot. One item of clothing many hunters overlook is buttons. I make sure none of my hunting clothes has buttons on the pockets before I go into the woods, because the bowstring may catch on that button when the string's released and throw off the shot. Although the problems I've mentioned may seem small, they do make the difference in shooting accurately.

PRACTICE FOR GREATER ACCURACY

The mind's ability to influence a hunter's shooting is almost magical. An old saying that's especially true in bowhunting is, "How you think, you are."

One of the most overlooked keys to shooting accurately is your confidence in yourself to shoot straight and true. You must know even before you draw the bow that you can take the deer. You can't just think you can bag the deer; you must be convinced that when the arrow is released, the deer in front of you is dead. To develop that kind of confidence in your shooting, you must spend hours practice shooting.

Practice at varying and unknown distances. After becoming an accurate shooter in your backyard from both a tree stand and on the ground, walk through the woods and shoot at random targets, such as stumps, fallen pine cones and other objects where the distance has not been predetermined. This exercise will teach you to judge distance and learn how to aim at varying distances quickly and easily.

Also carry your tree stand into the woods before the season, and shoot at targets at unknown distances. One of the major reasons bowhunters miss their deer is because they can't judge how far they are from the animals they're trying to take. When you're 15- to 20-feet up in a tree, distances can be quite deceptive. Even a 5-yard error in judgment can spell disaster.

POSITION YOUR TREE STAND PROPERLY

An important factor in making a lethal shot is the height of your tree stand. I never place my tree stand more than 15 to 20 feet high -- and certainly not 30 to 40 feet high. The higher you climb, the more you increase the angle of flight the arrow takes to get to the deer, and the smaller your target effectively becomes.

If you're 30-feet high and a deer is 10 to 15 yards out from the base of the tree, there's no way the arrow can penetrate through both of the deer's lungs. More than likely the broadhead will hit one lung and go over or under the other. You are far better off placing your arrow so that it penetrates both lungs and comes out the other side of the deer.

I realize deer are more likely to see you if you're closer to the ground, and your scent probably will be easier for the deer to pick up than if you are higher in the tree. However, if you spend more time camouflaging yourself and your silhouette and hunt into the wind, I'm convinced the advantages of positioning your stand lower in the tree outweigh the advantages of being higher in the tree.

Noel Feather of Sterling, IL, has killed two Boone & Crockett bucks with his bow. He has tested his equipment and has the confidence to know his arrow will fly straight to the target.

When you spot the deer coming toward your tree stand, several things you can do will help prepare you for the shot. As soon as I see an animal coming, I pick up my bow -- my arrow already is nocked -- stand up, face the deer and wait for the right opportunity to shoot. If the deer gets too close, it may see you when you stand. Be prepared.

As the deer continues to approach, I slowly move into a good shooting position. I also try and guess where the deer will be when I do have the opportunity to shoot. If the deer is walking toward an opening or a break in the cover, then I want to make sure that when the deer reaches that spot I'm ready to shoot. Another reason for getting into shooting position before the deer is close enough to shoot is because every tree stand I've ever used has at least one squeak in it that inevitably occurs when a deer is close by.

If I have to make some final adjustments when the buck's within bow range, I make the adjustments slowly and deliberately. Then, even if the deer spots me, usually I won't spook him. If a deer within bow range looks at me, I won't take the shot; he's liable to jump the string if he sees your release. Never take a bad shot. If a deer walks within range but you're

If the broadhead flies straight to the target, most broadheads will bring down a buck.

not confident of making a lethal shot, then don't shoot. Instead, hunt that deer another day.

To determine your killing range, learn at what distance you can put six arrows consistently in a bull's-eye. Since for me that's 40 yards, I consider my killing range to be 40 yards. However, at 30 yards or less, I'm much more accurate. Within 20 yards, I think I can kill anything that

When the buck presents himself for a shot, if the arrow doesn't fly straight, then all your hunting and your practice shooting will be in vain.

walks. Even though my killing range is 40 yards, I'll rarely take a shot at more than 30 yards. I have no excuse for missing a deer at 20 yards or less.

If your sight pins are set at 40, 30, 20 and 10 yards, be sure to practice shooting the middle distances of 35, 25 and 15 yards. You may be accurate at 30 yards yet miss a deer at 25 because you haven't practiced shooting at distances in between the distances for which your sight pins are set.

There's a time when the deer comes to within your killing range that you know you can take the animal, and that's when you should shoot. Although I say never to take an iffy shot, I also believe you rarely get the perfect shot. When the animal is positioned such that you know you can make a clean kill, take the shot. If you don't, chances are very good you may not get another opportunity. The wind may change directions, the deer may smell you, another deer may spook your deer, or any number of factors can cause the deer to leave.

When a buck is within 40 yards, I know I can arrow him. But if he continues to move closer, I won't shoot until he gets to within 20 yards. I like a 20-yard shot. Since I always shoot for the lungs, I prefer a broadside shot or a quartering shot, where I can slip the arrow in behind the last rib, and the shaft will move straight forward through the deer.

Once you're at full draw, and your sight reaches your aiming point, don't attempt to hold the bow still for a long time. When your pin settles on the spot, let the "automatic system" you use to shoot accurately while practicing take over. You'll feel yourself making the lethal hit just as the arrow is being released.

After my release, I still concentrate on the arrow. Most of the time I actually can watch the arrow hit the deer. With the fast bows everyone is shooting today, seeing the arrows hit the deer is often difficult. But if you concentrate and don't flinch, you should see it strike the deer.

Your hit should be solid enough to penetrate through both sides of the animal, giving you two holes, which will leave a heavy blood trail. After the hit, watch the direction in which the animal runs, listen for him to fall, and mentally mark the last place you saw him so you can start trailing him.

UNDERSTAND THE IMPORTANCE OF EXPERIENCE

One of the reasons many bowhunters don't bag more trophy bucks is because they don't have experience taking many deer -- or any deer -- when the buck of a lifetime appears. Often we're too eager to become trophy hunters before we become good bowhunters. I believe you should have taken at least 10 to 20 deer before you decide to become a trophy hunter. There's nothing wrong with bagging does with a bow in the states that permit either-sex hunting. Actually, taking several unantlered deer with a bow can help build you confidence. Then if a buck does appear, you know how to settle your nerves, concentrate and make the shot.

Build the confidence you need to shoot at a trophy buck. Then, when and if you see a trophy deer in the woods, you'll have the confidence from those previous kills to draw upon. Also, remember that trophy only may come along once or twice in a lifetime. Why limit the sport of bowhunting to only taking those one or two deer? Developing your skill in harvesting deer and enjoying the sport of bowhunting for many years will be far more rewarding than bagging that one trophy buck of a lifetime.

Although there's no great secret to shooting accurately, a bowhunter must remember many small details. Be more conscious about these details. Then you'll consistently take more deer.

CHAPTER 5

ARE TREE STANDS FRIENDS OR FOES?

When you fall out of a tree and before you hit the ground, you have plenty of time to think about the mistakes you've made and what you should have done to prevent the beating you're about to take. I know from firsthand experience. I've fallen from tree stands on four different occasions, although not in recent years. The bruises, scratches, scrapes and loss of breath finally have taught me how important learning tree stand safety is and how to keep from falling when I climb.

I remember the first Baker tree stand I ever saw. In those days, you hugged a tree and pulled the stand up with your feet. You had to be somewhat of an athlete with both upper and lower body strength to use a climbing stand. But getting into the tree was not nearly as difficult as staying in it.

In the early days of tree stand construction, "store-bought" tree stands were expensive. Everyone I knew thought they could build a better tree stand for less money than the ones being offered on the market. Most of the early backyard tree stand manufacturers had little or no knowledge of what was required to make a tree stand safe. They didn't know any of the properties of the types of metal they were using. None of these stands came with an instruction book or safety tips. The standard phrase all deer hunters used in those early days was, "If you go up into a tree with a climbing tree stand, sooner or later you will come down the tree faster than you want to and at a time you least expect."

According to one of the nation's leading tree stand manufacturers, Ray McIntyre, president of Warren and Sweat Manufacturing Company, "About 10 tree stand-related fatalities will occur each year. Also about 600 tree stand injuries will happen per year in 30 states that will result in lost-time injuries. Ninety percent of all these fatalities and injuries would have been preventable if the hunter had worn a safety belt."

THE MOST DANGEROUS STANDS

Certain types of tree stands have accident written all over them. As McIntyre explained, "Eighty-five percent of the accidents that occur with

Tree stands are one of the greatest inventions ever created for bowmen.

tree stands are the result of a hunter using a homemade stand. The most dangerous kinds of stands are constructed of wood. When a hunter nails 2x4 steps or wooden blocks to a tree to climb into that tree, he's building for himself and others a potential accident.

"When you drive nails through the center of wood, you split or weaken that wood. After a year or two, that wood begins to rot, as does the holes around the nails, causing the steps to be unsafe and to break away from the tree easily. Wooden steps and wooden ladders pose the biggest dangers to the tree stand hunter."

Also if you build a wooden tree stand, you must realize the life of wooden tree stands generally is no more than one to two years, unless the stands are built of an expensive grade of marine plywood. If you want to save money in tree stand construction and think wood is the answer, face the fact that you're possibly constructing an accident for yourself or others who use that stand.

TREE STEPS

Tree steps also can pose a potential threat to those who bow hunt. The steps themselves are not unsafe. But if you don't attach the steps to the tree properly, an accident can occur.

"For a screw-in type step to offer the safest passage from the ground to the tree, the step must be screwed all the way into the tree to make if flush against the tree," McIntyre emphasized. "Most hunters will screw the first two or three steps tightly into the tree. However, as they climb higher and become tired, they often don't take those last two or three turns on the step to screw it all the way into the tree. Generally the steps most likely to break away from the tree will be the top steps, because the hunter has tired of screwing steps into the tree as he climbs towards his stand."

If you fall out of a tree when you use tree steps and fall away from the tree, you may not be hurt as badly as when you fall straight down beside the tree.

"When you fall down besides a tree with tree steps, those steps can catch rings or other jewelry, an arm or a leg and produce a nasty cut or possibly pull off body parts," McIntyre reported. "Always take the extra time required to make sure that the last few steps at the top are as secure to the tree as the first step at the bottom."

Another problem with utilizing tree steps is you may shortchange yourself on the number of steps you screw into a tree. You may use only enough steps to allow you to climb to your stand. Then from the last step, you may come from below your stand to try and get into the stand.

"When you approach a tree stand from below or from the side of the stand, the chances of pushing the stand away from the tree are much greater than if you come from above the stand and step down into it," McIntyre said. "If you'll use two to three more tree steps to climb above the stand to enable you to step down into your stand, the likelihood of an accident will be reduced."

49

Many states require rope-on or belt-on types of tree steps instead of the screw-in kind to prevent damaging the tree. These belt-on steps can be safer than the screw-in type. However, you still must remember when you're attaching the steps to the tree to make sure the rope holding the step is parallel to the ground. Also pull the step securely to the tree with no slack in the rope. If slack is in the rope, the step can slide down the tree when weight is applied to it.

No matter what type of step you utilize to climb into your tree stand, as soon as you leave the steps and enter the stand, attach a safety belt. If you walk out onto the end of the stand and rock the stand back and forth to be certain the stand is stable against the tree before you attach your safety belt, you may take an unexpected express ride to the bottom.

CLIMBING TREE STANDS

Climbing tree stands are much safer than tree steps and fixed stands because you are less exposed to danger. The climbing stands that surround the hunter in some type of metal cage are the safest of all. However, you must take safety precautions.

"When you fasten a climbing tree stand to the tree, you must realize that most trees are bell-shaped -- larger at the bottom than they are at the top," McIntyre reported. "When you attach the seat and the platform, make sure both parts of the stand are leaning into the tree slightly. The more tapered the tree is, the more you should have the tree stand leaning into the tree before you start your climb."

Although when the words, "tree stand accidents," are heard most of us think of someone falling from a great height to the ground, some accidents occur at less than three feet off the ground.

"A hunter may fall out of a climbing tree stand when he's attaching the ropes or the bungee cords to his feet to enable him to pull the stand up as he climbs," McIntyre mentioned. "When you're standing up in a tree stand trying to attach footstraps, you're in an awkward position. Falling can be easy. When you attach the straps to your feet, always be seated in the stand first to greatly reduce your chance for accidents."

McIntyre is a firm believer in the use of safety belts -- even when you're climbing with your tree stand. Statistics have proven that safety belts can prevent as many if not more accidents for hunters as seat belts do for drivers of automobiles.

"Before you start to climb the tree in a climbing tree stand, attach your safety belt to the tree," McIntyre explained. "As you climb, slide the belt up the tree, and move the belt above you. Then you're always secure to the tree from the time you leave the ground."

Once you arrive at the desired height, either use the strap securing

Climbing tree stands have enabled more archers to get into trees safely to bag deer.

your feet to the bottom platform, or carry a piece of rope to tie the seat climber to the bottom platform. Then if the bottom half of the stand comes loose from the tree and falls, it can't fall any further than the length of rope you have attached to it. Also this bottom platform can be retrieved easily to allow you to come down the tree safely. If and when you stand in the tree stand, make sure your safety belt is attached snugly.

LADDER STANDS

The safest type of ladder stands are the ones with a brace about six feet up in the middle of the ladder to brace the center of the ladder to the tree. This brace usually can be secured to the tree before you begin to climb the ladder. Also have a strap or a chain at the top of the ladder stand to secure the stand to the tree.

"I like a ladder tree stand that has a belt and ratchet system to allow me to not only secure a ladder type stand to the tree but also actually pull the stand in tighter to the tree and make the stand more secure," McIntyre commented.

Remember, when you get to the top of the ladder to fasten your safety belt to the tree to prevent your possibly falling from the ladder.

SAFETY BELTS

All types of safety belts are available on the market today. The most common belt is a wide nylon strap that can be secured to the tree and then slipped over your head and secured to your chest. These belts are lightweight and easy to use and will prevent you from falling to the ground.

A good safety harness can save your life when bowhunting from a tree stand.

However, from field testing these kinds of belts, I've also learned they have some inherent problems.

Many hunters put the belts around their waists instead of around their chests. If you slide the belt around your waist like a hangman's noose, then when you fall that belt will continue to tighten up and squeeze you in the middle. Also, if you use a safety belt attached only at your waist, if and when you fall, there's a good chance you may hang upside down in the tree. Although hanging upside down is uncomfortable, righting yourself can be almost impossible. If you don't fall to the ground, you may have incurred another problem -- how to get out of your safety belt when you're upside-down.

To solve this problem, grab hold of the tree with your arms, and right yourself. Next wrap your arms and your legs around the tree, and climb up to loosen the belt. Continue to climb up or down until you reach your stand or the ground.

Two of the safest, most comfortable safety belts I've used are the Hide 'Um Hunter harness from Brell Mar and the Warren and Sweat Safety Harness, which perform several useful tasks. When wearing these safety harnesses, if you fall out of a tree, your weight is distributed at your waist and shoulders because the straps form an "H" pattern across your upper body. I have hung in these harnesses while field testing them. Although hanging from a strap isn't comfortable, I have found them much more comfortable than the single-strap safety belts most of us utilize.

I also have learned I'm less likely to hang upside down in these harnesses than when I use a safety belt that only wraps around my chest.

The most dangerous type of tree stand is a wooden, permanent stand like this one.

Yet another advantage to this safety harness is I feel much more secure with the shoulder straps and the waist strap when I have to lean out from the tree to take a shot with my bow than I do when I lean out with only a chest strap to secure me to the tree.

Too, if you take a deer, dragging the animal out with the harness is easier than trying to pull the deer out by either his antlers or his legs. By attaching the strap that is designed to go around the tree to the deer's head or antlers, you can stand upright and lean forward, straining against the harness, to drag the deer out. This type of harness allows you to use your back and leg muscles to pull the deer and frees-up your hands to carry your gun and/or other equipment. Although I'm sure there are other fine safety belts on the market, I have found this safety-type harness to be the most comfortable and user-friendly type of safety belt/deer drag available.

THE LAST WORD ON TREE STAND SAFETY

In many states, you are required to take a hunter safety course before you can obtain a hunting license. These safety courses, which try to prevent hunter fatalities and accidents in the woods, have been very effective in making the woods safer for all of us.

However, I feel some type of hunter safety course should be required for anyone hunting from a tree stand. We all think we know how to be safe in a tree stand. But remember, of the more than 600 tree stand-related accidents each year, none involved believed they would fall out of tree stands. They thought they knew how to be safe when actually they didn't.

To help accident-proof you and your hunting companions, obtain a copy of the tree stand safety video offered by Warren and Sweat Manufacturing. This video demonstrates how to correctly use each type of tree stand, reviews the safety points associated with each stand and shows where accidents can happen if the stands are used improperly. This one video may save your life or the lives of your hunting friends.

Hunting from a tree stand is one of the most effective ways for you to see and bag deer when hunting with your bow. However, when you leave the ground and move up a tree, you can be in harm's way unless you take the proper precautions.

CHAPTER 6

AVOID THE COMMON MISTAKES BOWHUNTERS MAKE

Good bowhunters can be better bowhunters if they don't commit sins that decrease their odds for bagging any deer and especially trophy deer. Following are 10 of the most common mistakes, according to Noel Feather, that even good bowhunters -- sportsmen who have taken several deer with a bow and who have hunted for four or five years -- make.

STARTING TO TROPHY HUNT TOO QUICKLY

Most bowmen want to be trophy hunters. Once a bowhunter gets into the sport and begins to read about Boone and Crockett or Pope and Young trophy deer and about the archers who take these kinds of animals, he sets a goal for himself to become a trophy hunter. However, most of these sportsmen don't put in the hours or take enough deer to become good hunters -- much less trophy hunters.

I think these hunters are making a very big mistake and missing out on a lot of fun. As a trophy hunter, the outdoorsman may hunt all season and not even see a Pope and Young set of antlers. A buck must have extremely large antlers to make the book. A bowhunter may search his entire life for a trophy deer that's Boone and Crockett size and never find it. He'll have to let numbers of nice deer walk by without ever harvesting them.

One of the best reasons for becoming a bowhunter is to take deer with a bow. Bagging deer with a bow is what the sport is all about. Therefore the hunter who becomes a trophy hunter too quickly misses the best of bowhunting, because he's so obsessed with taking a trophy.

Another problem associated with becoming a trophy hunter too soon is if a bowhunter hasn't bagged quite a few deer with a bow, I don't believe he'll be mentally ready to take a trophy, even if the shot presents itself. If the hunter's ever going to have shaking knees and shortness of breath before a shot and be so nervous he can't hold his bow steady -- it will happen when a big set of antlers comes into bow range. Only by learning to deal with the emotional problems directly affecting arrow flight in the

Many hunters, especially trophy hunters, are waiting for that perfect day to go out and bag a buck.

woods can the hunter expect to be successful. Only by taking numbers of deer can the hunter learn to control his emotions at this moment of truth.

I think the bowhunter who wants to become a trophy hunter should have bagged at least six to 10 deer with his bow before he tries to become a trophy hunter, and 20 deer would be even better. In my opinion, this idea of being a trophy hunter has been overplayed. I don't think everybody should hope to be a trophy hunter.

I don't consider trophy hunting the ultimate in bowhunting. I do it because I like it, and I've taken enough deer with my bow I want to attempt to bag bigger deer. Although I still enjoy taking a doe or a smaller buck, for me, the most satisfying hunt is for the big, smart, trophy deer. However, I don't think an archer must become a trophy hunter to be a good bowhunter.

SHOOTING TOO QUICK OR WAITING TOO LONG

Many good bowhunters don't harvest deer as often as they can because they don't know when to take their shots. They either shoot before they have a good shot or wait for the best shot and never get a shot.

Experience is the best teacher a bowhunter can have, because a hunter must learn when he should take a shot. But my rule is that when an animal presents me with a good shot that I feel I can put him down with, that's the time I shoot. I don't believe you ever should hurry a shot. However, also I've found that you shouldn't wait on that best shot, because many times deer won't give you the shot for which you're looking. I've waited around for that best shot before, never had it presented to me and watched a nice deer walk away from me. Don't play with a deer, don't watch a deer, and don't take a head-on shot either. But when you've got a good shot, take it.

IGNORING THE WIND

Even though a bowhunter is experienced and understands he should hunt with the wind in his face, often you'll be surprised how many hunters think they can cheat and hunt in an area -- even though the wind's wrong. My number one rule is no matter how good a hunting site is or how excellent I think my chances are of taking a buck in that spot, if the wind's not in my favor, I won't hunt that region. But instead I'll go to where I believe my chances may not be as good but where I can hunt with a favorable wind.

Of course since many bowhunters are convinced they can kill deer, they may tell themselves, ''I know the wind's wrong, but I'm going ahead and hunt that stand, because I just know I can kill a deer in there today.'' However, probably nine times out of 10, they won't kill a deer and will have fouled up the area with their human scent in the process.

OVERUSING A STAND

I've found tree stands can be and often are overhunted. If I hunt a stand in the morning as well as in the afternoon, then I won't go to that stand the next day. If you hunt from the same stand over and over again, the deer wise up to what you're doing. You're leaving scent going to and from the stand and on and around the tree as you climb up and down.

Particularly when hunting trophy whitetails, the less exposure they have to human odor, the better your odds are of taking them. The more

57

exposure the deer have to human odor, the less chance the hunter will have to bag a specific buck. Deer wise up to a hunter's movement patterns quickly. The only advantage the archer really has for taking a smart deer is to be in a spot where the deer doesn't expect him to be. Therefore the more times a deer smells human odor, the more likely the animal will be to avoid that area. Consequently, the more times you hunt from the same stand, the less effective that stand will be in producing a deer.

CONTROLLING BODY ODOR

Notice I'm not advocating eliminating body odor. Dead folks are the only people who don't have body odor. However, the hunter can control how much odor he emits. Many hunters don't pay enough attention to body odor control, which begins with taking a shower each day.

Besides keeping the body clean, make every effort to have clean clothes. In my opinion, having clean clothes does not solely mean keeping the clothes dirt-free but more importantly odor-free. If you store your hunting clothes in your house, the clothes you hunt in will pick up smells of deodorizers, food, cooking and pets. I recommend storing your clothes you'll wear hunting in a plastic bag in the vehicle you'll use. Then put your clothes on just before you hunt.

Be sure not to store clothes in your hunting club, because the night before a hunt there probably will be woods smoke from the fireplace as well as tobacco smoke and food smells from breakfast cooking. Having those odors in your clothes can alarm the deer you're hoping to take. One of the worst things you can do if you come in from hunting with wet clothes is to hang those clothes in front of an open fireplace to dry out and then plan to hunt in those same clothes that afternoon. Your hunting clothes may be dry, but they're also full of every odor in the lodge. I'm convinced deer can detect those odors.

I like a dog as much as anybody. But when I get ready to go hunting and put on my clothes, I don't want a dog rubbing up against me. I don't want to pet him. I don't want him around me, because I know deer don't like dogs.

Be sure to leave your boots in your hunting vehicle too, not in the house. Hunting clothes are designed to wear in the woods while a sportsman is hunting. Other clothes are made to wear in a house or a hunting lodge.

OVERDRESSING

The hunter has two problems with body odor and body heat as they relate to hunting. He must wear enough clothes to stay warm as he walks to his tree stand. But if he wears too many clothes and perspires while he's walking, then the clothes have caused him to sweat. Also, the evaporation of moisture from the sweat actually makes him cold. If the hunter sweats

Some of the worst days of the year seem to be the most productive for Noel Feather.

heavily as he walks to his stand in his warm clothes, then he's like a radiator, giving off human odor in all directions along the path he walks. Many hunters overdress when walking to their stands.

When I'm hunting in cold weather, I wear insulated clothing and insulated underwear. If I put my goose down vest on and walk maybe a mile to my tree stand, by the time I arrive there, I'll be sweating and giving off too much human odor. This problem keeps me from hunting deer with any confidence at all, and within 30-minutes, I'll be cold too. Even if a deer does come in, I won't be comfortable or able to shoot accurately.

In my opinion, the bowhunter needs two types of clothing -- the clothing he wears when he walks to his stand and warmer, heavier clothing he carries in a pack and doesn't actually put on until he reaches his stand. By using this system of dressing, the hunter will not give off nearly as much human odor and will be able to hunt warmer and more comfortably then if he wears all that clothing into his tree stand.

Even if you're wearing a human scent cover-up but are sitting in a tree stand sweating, the best cover-up scents aren't going to be able to hide the human odor you're giving off. To put it simply, I haven't found any cover-up scent that can mask the human odor of a sweaty body.

NOT KNOWING WHERE TO PUT LURE

Most hunters are very excited about all the new lures and scents on the market today. However, many good bowhunters don't understand the difference in a cover-up scent and a deer lure. A cover-up scent or a masking scent is used to help disguise human odor and is not meant to attract deer. Therefore these scents are best pinned to, poured on or wiped over the sportsman's outer clothing.

A deer lure is a substance that's made and designed to attract deer. In other words, when the deer smells the lure, the deer is supposed to come in looking for whatever gives off that odor. For example, a lure like doe-in-estrus is produced for the hunter to put around his stand to hopefully cause a buck to come into the area searching for the estrous doe that's urinated in that spot. If the buck comes in looking for the doe, and the hunter has put buck lure on his body, then the deer will be looking for the hunter. The deer's nose shows the deer's eyes where to search for the critter that gives off the odor. If a bowhunter in a tree stand smells like an estrous doe, that buck will come in and look up that tree for the doe that surely must have climbed it. He'll spot the hunter, spook, and run.

To use a buck lure effectively, leave the buck lure on the ground or at eye level to the deer. Then when the buck comes in, he's looking at the lure and not at the hunter.

Another mistake hunters make with buck lure is they place it on their feet, the soles of their shoes or the cuffs of their pants and then walk into the woods. If a deer crosses that path and smells the lure, and the hunter is facing into the wind and has walked into the wind to go to his stand, then when the buck follows that lure scent, he will walk up behind the hunter. Then he will look up into the tree where the strongest scent is coming from and spot the archer. If you're planning to utilize any type of scent on the soles of your feet or the cuffs of your pants, be sure it's a cover-up scent. Only put out buck lure where you want the buck to show up, and only place it in a spot where you want him to look.

NOT UNDERSTANDING WHEN TO RATTLE

Most experienced bowhunters know rattling can be an effective tool to call in a buck, but many of them believe that the best time to rattle is during the peak of the rut. The rut occurs at the same time every year in a given area. Why, you even can plan your vacation for next year for the rut, because the rut is controlled by the shortness of the day and the amount of light that enters a deer's eye. Generally the same amount of light will be present on December 22 every year in a specific region. If that happens to be the day that's the peak of the rut in your region this year, there's a very good chance that same day next year will be the peak of the rut too.

To use a grunt call successfully, you must understand the reasons deer respond to a call.

Although oldtimers believed a cold snap touched off the rut, all that usually happens during a cold snap is deer become more active. I think deer are just more comfortable in cold weather since they have hollow hair and are well-insulated. I believe the deer may be uncomfortable when the weather's hot. But the time of the rut does not change in an area.

Remember, the buck is ready to breed as soon as he comes out of the velvet. But he's not going to breed until the doe is ready to be bred. Bucks are in the woods waiting on that first estrous doe to come into heat. I believe that rattling or using a grunt call two weeks before the rut begins is the most effective way to call in a buck. When that old boy is in the woods listening and hears horns clashing, he thinks to himself, ''Somebody out there has found a hot doe, and while they're fighting over her, I'll move in and breed her.'' Or, he hears a grunt call, and he may think, ''Some deer is tending an estrous doe. Maybe there's two of those does, and I can move in and breed one before anyone notices.''

Just after the rut, the buck is looking for a late bloomer, a doe that will come into rut after the other does have. Therefore using rattling horns and grunt calls two weeks after the rut also can be very productive. During

61

the peak of the rut, many bucks will have does with them. Then they may be less likely to come to rattling horns or grunt calls.

NOT BEING ALERT IN THE STAND

Many outdoorsmen brag about how long they sit in their tree stands waiting on deer to show up. But if the hunter is in his stand either asleep, daydreaming or not hunting (actively trying to see and take a deer), then the length of time he spends suspended between heaven and earth has no direct bearing on his success as a bowhunter.

Many good bowhunters make the mistake of staying in a tree stand when they're not hunting. When you catch yourself falling asleep or not actively looking for deer, the best thing you can do is leave the tree stand and come out of the woods. When a sportsman's hunting, he should be hunting. When he's resting, he should be resting somewhere other than the woods. Often during those rest times is when a deer is most likely to appear. If the hunter is not alert and anticipating seeing a deer, he's more likely to shoot too quickly or inaccurately, or make noise and spook the deer.

WAITING ON A PERFECT DAY

Many hunters, especially trophy hunters, are waiting on that perfect day to go out and try and bag a buck. They come up with excuses for not hunting like the weather's too hot or too cold, or there's too much wind or not enough wind. But I've learned the perfect day to hunt a trophy buck is any day you can go into the woods. The more days you are in the woods, the greater your chances of bagging a trophy.

One of the biggest bucks I ever took, which was a Boone and Crockett buck, I harvested on a morning with so much wind I almost didn't go. I hate to hunt in the wind. But because the weather was so windy, the buck probably never heard me as I approached my stand. He came in quickly and easily.

Just remember, you can't take a buck -- any buck -- sitting at home watching TV or drinking a cup of coffee. You must be in the woods.

CHAPTER 7

SOLVE THE DIFFICULT PROBLEMS OF BOWHUNTING

Bowhunters can find all types of excuses for not hunting, for why hunting is difficult and for what keeps them from being successful. Let's look at some bowhunting situations with Bob Foulkrod, who is recognized as a master bowhunter, discuss how to deal with these problems, and see if we can improve our chances for taking whitetails.

BOWHUNTING IN THE RAIN

According to Foulkrod, "When the rain is pouring down, most bowhunters can come up with all kinds of excuses for not hunting:

• 'I won't be able to climb the tree in the rain,'
• 'I won't be able to see the deer,'
• 'My fingers will slip on the string,'
• 'I won't be able to track a deer if I do arrow one,' and/or
• 'Raingear is too noisy to permit me to stand and take a shot if I do see a deer,' etc.

"Probably the number one excuse for not hunting in the rain is the hunter thinks the deer aren't going to move, but this assumption is just not true. I believe the hunters who use this for an excuse must think deer go inside and lie up near a fire when the rains come. However, whitetails are accustomed to the elements and do move and feed during a rain.

"Where I hunt in the East, most of our shots are from 10 to 20 yards. Naturally one of the most critical keys to success is having quiet raingear. Since raingear is noisy, if you don your raingear, wait for a deer to come in range, and then stand and take a shot, more than likely the suit that keeps you dry will be responsible for running off and spooking your deer.

"I wear my rainsuit and then either put on cotton clothing or some type of polar fleece clothing on top of my rainsuit. Although my outside clothing will get wet, I'll stay dry with the outside clothing muffling the raingear. The other option bowmen have is not to wear any raingear at all and get thoroughly soaked but remain quiet.

"When a deer is standing immediately under my stand, I usually wait for him to take one or two more steps and don't attempt to shoot straight down," Bob Foulkrod explains.

"Yet another problem that prevents many hunters from facing the elements on a rainy day is they reason that if they arrow a deer, the rain will wash away the blood trail before they can locate the animals. To prevent this from happening, I use a Game Tracker, which consists of a spool of string that mounts on the front of the bow. The string attaches to the arrow. When the arrow is released, the string flies with the arrow to the target. As the deer runs off, the string feeds out of the Game Tracker and leaves a trail to the deer. Even if the string breaks, it still shows the direction of flight the deer has taken.

"Most of my hunters shoot at 20 yards or less. Although some may say the Game Tracker may affect the flight of the arrow, I don't believe the string inhibits the flight of the arrow at that distance enough to be noticeable. Also to track deer on a rainy day, I advise hunters to get down from their tree stands and trail the deer as soon as they arrow them.

"Another misconception about hunting on a rainy day is that the hunter has to use vanes instead of feathers for his fletchings. However, I always hunt with feathers, because I'm only going to shoot the arrow one time. Therefore the fletchings aren't going to have a chance to get as matted or tangled as they will if you are target shooting and have to shoot the same arrow several times.

"If you're stalk hunting, you must be careful not to get your fletchings up against brush or bushes that can cause a problem with the fletchings. Although many hunters have suggested spraying fletchings with silicone, I believe deer have learned to relate that silicone smell to the hunter. If you utilize silicone, you may spook the deer you're trying to hunt. I don't put anything on my feathers and haven't found that I have any problem shooting them in the rain."

HUNTING DRY WEATHER

"Hunting during dry weather conditions just about eliminates stalk hunting," Foulkrod explains. "But you do have to walk going to and away from your stand, which can spook deer. Remember, a man has a definite cadence to his step. A deer, however, has four feet, which makes a deer's cadence altogether different from a man's. A deer often sounds like two men walking through the woods rather than one.

"One of the ways to disguise your approach to and from your stand is to take smaller and more steps than you ordinarily do. Then you'll sound more like a deer than a man. Another technique is to let a stick drag behind you as you walk, which also breaks up the rhythm of your walking. Your best bet during dry weather conditions is to spend as little time as you possibly can walking and as much time as you can in a tree."

TAKING THE LONG SHOT AND WHEN NOT TO

"Most bowhunters are going to take a shot at 30 yards or less," Foulkrod says. "However, occasionally a big buck will come in at 40 yards. Then the sportsman must make the decision whether or not to take the shot.

"In my opinion, the only way a hunter ever should take that 40-yard shot is if he's been practicing at that distance for a long time and knows for certain he can make that shot. The hunter must be convinced that shot is not a gamble. If the sportsman is only 50-percent accurate at 40 yards shooting at a paper target, then he has no business taking that shot. If you take into account all the factors that affect a sportsman when he's shooting at a deer rather than when he's aiming at paper, the percentages are cut in half. Then the archer is probably only 25-percent effective at that range.

"Also remember if the deer hears you draw the bow, he may take a step or move just as you prepare to shoot. The deer's movement may mean you may have to hold the bow longer than you anticipated, which will cut your accuracy tremendously to resight or wait for a better shot. Ninety percent of the time, if you take that 40-yard shot, more than likely, you'll have a wounded animal you won't recover. Most good bowhunters I know can't live with that thought. If you have questions about taking a long shot, don't shoot."

BAGGING A DEER UNDER YOUR TREE STAND

"One of the most difficult shots for most bowhunters to take is when a deer is standing directly under their tree stands," Foulkrod reports. "Most bowmen can't make these shots because they don't practice shooting from this position. Most of the time when people are practicing, they have their legs spread apart, they draw the bows over their heads, and they shoot at targets in front of them.

"To be a proficient bowhunter who bags deer from a tree stand, I believe the archer should practice taking his shots with his feet spaced no wider apart than the tree stand. Also I think he should practice drawing his bow by pointing it at the ground and then bringing it up to the target, which requires less movement but does involve another set of muscles than when you're drawing the bow and pointing it at the sky. Another advantage to drawing the bow by pointing it at the ground is the only movement this entails is pulling the string back. In other words, you don't have to pull the bow up over your head, draw it and begin to back it down to aim at the deer.

"Another mistake many archers make when they try to shoot a deer standing under a tree is they aim for the spot where they want the arrow to enter the deer and not for the place where they want the arrow to penetrate and eventually stop. In other words, if a deer is standing at an awkward angle, the hunter may have to take a shot which will require the arrow to pass through the stomach to get to the lungs. But this may be a better shot than trying to shoot for the shoulder where the arrow will hit the shoulder blade and possibly bounce off.

"When I aim, I attempt to look straight at the deer to the point where the arrow will hit. When the deer is standing right under my stand, I usually wait for him to take one or two more steps and don't attempt to shoot straight down on the deer's back in hopes of breaking the deer's spine and shooting through the deer's back. The target is just too small. If the deer is standing straight under you, and you're going to shoot for the backbone, I've found that usually you can wait and let the deer take one or two more steps away from the tree. Then you'll have a better target at which to shoot."

DETERMINING THE IMPORTANCE OF SCENTS, LURES AND CALLS

"I believe scents, lures and calls will work, if they're utilized at the proper time and under the right conditions," Foulkrod comments. "However, most people buy some type of deer attractant or deer call and never read the instructions which tell when and/or how to use the call or the attractant.

Bob Foulkrod Of Troy, Pennsylvania, has killed a world record caribou and 16 other caribou that qualify for the Pope & Young record book with his bow. He intensively hunts whitetails each year and has learned to solve bowhunting problems to bag more bucks.

"Even if the hunter plans to utilize rattling antlers, most good rattling antlers will come with a set of instructions telling the hunter when and when not to rattle. But many hunters just will buy a set of antlers, beat on them and then won't be able to understand why a deer won't come to them.

"One of the problems associated with using lures, calls and attractants is that in the East, most hunters only will have four, five or six Saturdays in which to hunt, which is the same time most other sportsmen in their areas will be hunting. Therefore instead of relying on his hunting skills, the typical hunter is looking for some type of gimmick he can use which will allow him to take his deer, before the other hunters bag their bucks. But the secret to hunting is there is no secret. Patience, woodsmanship and the ability to set your tree stand in the most productive place are the keys to consistently bagging deer with a bow."

SETTING UP A TREE STAND

"Many hunters will set up a tree stand and may see deer 50 yards from their stands all week long," Foulkrod mentions. "I'm convinced a hunter should move his tree stand -- even if he has to lose a hunting day to get his stand in the right place to take a deer -- rather than watching deer just out of range. I've also known other hunters, who after setting up their

When you let a stick drag along behind you, you break up the rhythm of your walking and don't spook as many deer.

tree stands, have sat in these stands for several weeks and not spotted any deer. If I set up a tree stand, I want to see deer.

"Although I don't believe the kill is the number one reason for bowhunting, I do go into the woods to attempt to bag a deer. If I can't take a deer, I at least want the opportunity to see deer. For all these people who say they go into the woods to observe wildlife while sitting in their tree stands, I suggest they go out on their front porches or down the road and stay out of the woods where other people are trying to hunt. Perhaps more bowhunters don't take more deer because they're reluctant to move their tree stands once they put them up."

If you have the wind in your favor, you may be able to stalk in close to a buck.

PREPARING POORLY EQUALS BAD LUCK

"One of the most difficult problems with taking deer from a tree stand is the noise the hunter makes when he stands to shoot, when he draws his bow, when he moves on the stand to shoot or when his clothes rustle against a bush," Foulkrod advises. "In my opinion, this is not bad luck but rather are hunting problems created by the hunter.

"Most bowmen believe when they put a stand in a tree that all that's left to do is to hunt from that tree stand. However, successful tree stand hunting involves much more than having an elevated platform from which to shoot. After I've placed a stand in a tree, I stand on that stand and practice drawing and aiming in every direction from which a deer possibly can come.

"If a limb or a twig may be in the way when a deer presents a shot, I eliminate it. If any branch is sticking out close to my seat, I cut it off. Then my clothes won't brush against it. If my tree stand squeaks the slightest bit, I try to locate the squeak and get rid of it. I try to eliminate all the excuses or all the problems that keep me from taking a clean shot once the deer presents that shot. This preparation is made prior to my actually hunting from that stand. When I leave a stand site, I know the next time I get in that stand, I've removed all the problems I can that will prevent me from taking a clean shot at a deer.''

ELIMINATING THE PROBLEM OF HOLDING TOO LONG

''Many hunters draw their bows as soon as the deer are within range and then attempt to hold their shots until the deer offer the perfect shot,'' Foulkrod says. ''But I believe often a deer's sixth sense lets the animal know when the hunter is going to take a shot. The longer a hunter holds a shot, the easier the deer can detect the shot, and the more likely the deer is to run off.

''Perhaps when a hunter draws a bow to shoot, he sends out a signal that's like a magnetic field notifying the deer of danger. Have you noticed when you've been hunting with the wind in your favor, and a doe in your region hasn't seen you but you've seen her, how many times she will be alerted to danger and walk stiff-legged through your area? I think perhaps she can feel the presence of the hunter. I never draw my bow until I'm ready to shoot. When I draw, I'm ready to loose the arrow.

''Too, never wait on the very best shot. I think oftentimes deer present three shots -- an iffy shot, a good shot and the best shot. I always take the good shot and never wait on the best shot, because many times the best shot never will appear. When I have a good shot I know I can make, I let the arrow fly.

''Something else I never do is look the deer in the eyes. Even if the deer doesn't see you, I think the deer's sixth sense notifies him of danger when you make eye contact with that deer. Then he realizes he's being watched. An older, smarter buck usually will back out of a region when this happens, while a doe or young buck may walk stiff-legged through the area. Once I see the deer and know he's a buck I want to take, I concentrate on the spot where I'm going to try and place the arrow on the deer's body, and I never look up at the deer's face.

''These tactics are ones I use to solve deer hunting problems. Utilizing this information will increase your odds for taking a deer this season.''

70

CHAPTER 8

MAKE IT HAPPEN IN A TREE STAND

Sitting in a tree stand all day and waiting for a deer to appear can be about as exciting as watching maple syrup pour out of a bucket in zero degree weather. However, some newer and better tactics have been developed in recent years which give you more control over your destiny and can make bowhunting for deer much more exciting than it has been in the past.

Until about 10 years ago, you had almost no control over the deer you bowhunted. You only could take a stand in an area where your research and scouting had led you to believe a deer might show up and pray the deer would appear.

However, today, with the new and exciting deer calls on the market, you have the ability to make a deer come to where you are, to cause the deer to hunt you and to make bucks show up that ordinarily may not have walked into your sight. Here's a look at some calling strategies that can make bowhunting deer more exciting, more fun and much more productive for you.

BLEAT -- RUN-AND-GUN

"I like to use the bleat call at the beginning of bow season to take does," Wil Primos, president of Primos Game Calls, said. "In Mississippi where I hunt, most of the landowners manage their deer herds to try and keep the herds in balance and their land at its carrying capacity. As part of their herd management program, a certain number of doe deer must be removed from the herd each season. The landowners encourage bowhunters to harvest the does at every opportunity. I've learned by using the bleat call, I quickly and effectively can bring does into my stand and take a shot."

According to Primos, he moves into an area, sets up his tree stand, climbs into his stand and gets ready for the shot. "Most of the time, you will call a deer within five to 10 minutes after you've gotten into your stand. Before I start calling, I already have my arrow nocked and my fingers on the string.

71

Most of the time you will call a deer within 5 to 10 minutes after you've gotten in your stand.

"Once I give the bleat call, I start looking and listening for deer. As soon as I hear a deer running to my stand, I pull the arrow, bring the bow to full draw and anchor my shot. I know that in only a few seconds a doe will appear at my stand. When you call does in using a bleat call, they come in quickly. Then when they get out 15 to 20 yards from you, they start looking for the fawn that has made the bleat call. When they don't see the fawn, they'll leave as rapidly as they've come. Usually you'll only have two to six seconds to get your shot off. You won't have time to draw your bow and release it when the doe stops."

If the deer doesn't come within 10 minutes, Primos moves his stand 100 to 200 yards away and repeats the same process. One of the best ways to see this tactic in action is in Primos' video, "The Truth About Deer Hunting, No. II."

Eddie Salter, two-time World Turkey Calling Champion and the president of Eddie Salter Calls, attacks bowhunting for deer during the early season as aggressively as he goes after the wily gobblers in the spring.

"I enjoy hunting aggressively," Salter explained. "I like to make things happen. If game won't come to me, I'll go after it. Using the bleat call, I can hunt aggressively for deer just like I do turkey. In the spring of the year, if I go to an area in the woods and call and a turkey doesn't answer, then I continue to move through the woods until I make a turkey gobble. When a turkey gobbles, I hunt that bird.

"When I'm using the bleat call, I may call from five or 10 different stand sites in one morning. I'll move into an area, usually near thick cover, where I assume does may be bedded-down. I go up a tree, get into my tree stand and call for no more than five to 10 minutes. If the does don't come to that bleat call in that time frame, then more than likely they're not going to respond. I get out of the tree and move 100 to 200 yards away and then call again. Using this run-and-gun tactic, I often can call in 10 to 15 does in a morning.

"Another time I use the bleat call is when I've been in the stand for several hours in the morning hunting a buck and I haven't seen a buck or maybe I haven't seen any deer at all. Then I usually tell myself, `O.K., Eddie, you haven't seen a buck, but you can bag a doe this morning.' I take out my bleat call and make the call. Oftentimes a doe will come in and present a shot. On many days, I take what would have been an unproductive hunt and produce a deer to arrow."

At the first of the season in the states that permit the harvesting of does, the bleat call can be deadly effective for calling in whitetails. However, as the season progresses, this distress call tends to become less productive.

73

When you start calling deer, be prepared for the animal to come in to your stand in a hurry.

Remember, the fawn bleat is a distress call of a young deer. Generally you will call in primarily does with this call. However, because the call causes a spontaneous and urgent reaction which brings the does in quickly when they hear it, you can move from location to location and hunt much quicker from many more regions in a day utilizing this call than you can using other calls. With this tactic, you can make deer come to you.

THROW THE CALL

Calling more frequently and being more aggressive with your calling will produce more bucks within bow range than calling less and calling slower will. But a problem associated with calling deer is when they begin to come to within bow range, they spot the hunter.

"If you're going to make it happen in a treestand, you've got to be totally camouflaged," Wayne Carlton, the president of Carlton Calls, emphasized. "To get a buck to within bow range, I wear full Trebark camouflage a matching headnet and gloves."

Another mistake you may make when bowhunting deer and using the grunt call is to hold the call straight out from your stand. Since deer have the ability to pinpoint where a sound comes from, make a cup out of your hand. Put it against the end of the call to direct the sound being produced by the call either to the left or the right -- much like a ventriloquist throws his voice into a box or a dummy. If you use this throwing-the-call tactic with deer, the deer will think the call's coming from a position on the ground near your stand -- instead of from your tree stand. Then the buck

Wil Primos, owner of Primos Game Calls, often uses a run-and-gun tactic.

should come in to your left or your right and present a broadside shot rather than coming straight to you, presenting a poor shot.

Always aim the barrel of your call at the ground. Start calling by pointing the barrel of the call to the left of your tree stand. Then as you give a long series of 10 to 20 short, fast, snappy grunts, point the barrel of the call at different locations on the ground all the way around the tree. Make the sound of the call move from left to right or right to left and from close to the tree out away from the tree.

If you've observed deer, you probably have noticed that very rarely will either a buck or a doe stand in one place and continue to grunt. Most of the time when deer grunt, they're walking. By throwing the call and making the call move around the tree, you present a more realistic picture to the deer you're trying to lure in of a buck and a doe walking around your tree rather than standing in one spot. A problem you may encounter when bowhunting for deer and using the grunt call is when the deer comes in close, he may hangup at 40 to 50 yards out and be unwilling to move in that last 10 to 20 yards that will put him in bow range.

Wayne Carlton said, "When a buck comes in and hangs up just out of the range of my Bear First Strike Bow, instead of blowing through the call, I inhale through the call. I give short, muffled grunts and try to make the sound spread out. Then it doesn't sound like it's coming from any one spot. Using this technique when a deer is in close often means I can pull the animal to within bow range."

75

GO GET THEM WITH A GRUNT

Each year we learn more about the language of the whitetail as we experiment with new tactics of calling. The latest research on deer calling tends to indicate that one of the most basic rules of using the grunt call has been overlooked by most of us.

David Hale, co-owner of Knight and Hale Game Calls, and Wayne Carlton both agree that if a deer can't hear your call, he won't come to it. Each of these men solves this problem with a different method of calling and hunting.

"I don't believe a deer can tell by the volume of the call that another deer could not make a grunt call that loud," Hale observed. "By calling louder, you can increase the distance at which deer can hear and respond to your call."

Based on this philosophy, Knight and Hale Game Calls have made the Magnum Grunter, which produces a louder grunt than most calls on the deer hunting market today. To increase the distance at which deer can hear calling even more, Hale uses the principles of thermodynamics and wind currents to break with tradition and extend his calling effectiveness.

"Heat rises in cold weather," Hale explained. "On cold days, the human body is warmer than the air around it outdoors. Since human odor is carried by heat molecules, then on very cold days, that odor must rise rather than fall. During the morning, an air current known as a thermal comes from the ground and moves upward. In the morning when the air current is moving up and the bowhunter's body is warm, the natural flow of his human odor will be up rather than down.

"To increase the odds of a thermal carrying my odor above the deer, I climb 20 to 30 feet up in a tree to bowhunt. Then I have three factors working in my favor to keep my human odor out of the deer's nostrils.

"Since my odor is above the deer, I now can break one of the basic rules of successful deer hunting. I can hunt with the wind at my back in this situation, because of the thermals moving from the ground upward, the heat generated by my body and the great height I am in the tree. I also can use the wind to carry my Magnum Grunter's sound two or three times further than normally it will be effective for calling deer. With this strategy, I greatly increase the distances at which I can call deer."

Carlton has found that the more he calls, the more opportunities he has to lure in deer to his stand site. The traditional tactic employed to call deer in with a grunt call is to call three or four times, wait 15 minutes and then call once more. However, Carlton has realized that during the 15 minutes he's not calling, a deer may pass through his effective calling range that he will miss when the deer never hears Carlton grunt.

Carlton has found that the more he calls, the more opportunities he has to lure in deer to his stand site.

"That's why I call about once every two or three minutes," Carlton explained. "Instead of making three long grunts, I'll give 20 to 30 short, choppy grunts and make my calling sequence last from 30 seconds to a full minute. Because I'm calling more and more excitedly, any buck that walks through the productive range of my calling can and will hear me grunting and will be far more likely to come in than if he walks through that same area and doesn't hear the call. Bucks can't come to calling they don't hear. I don't want to miss an opportunity to take a buck with my bow because I didn't call when the deer could hear me."

RATTLE BUCKS

Where you rattle bucks may be more important than when you rattle bucks. Using rattling antlers is a tried and true tactic for luring in bucks. Many believe rattling produces bucks only under certain conditions and at specific times. The standard philosophy concerning rattling has been in the past that rattling ...

- Pays off best in areas where the makeup of the deer herd is closer skewed to a 1:1 ratio of bucks to does,
- Works only during the breeding season,
- Calls in dominant bucks and
- Doesn't produce after the rut.

However, I've always learned there are no absolutes in hunting whitetail deer. When you try and make absolute statements on what will

One of the most important keys to rattling successfully when you're bowhunting is to know where the buck is before you begin to rattle. Then you will understand from which direction to expect him and, when you hear or see him coming, you'll have time to draw your bow.

and won't produce bucks, you're much like the high school football player who's convinced himself he can date any girl in the school. More than likely if he continues to ask for dates, he will be turned down more times than he thinks. Consider these known factors about rattling:

• Bucks spar from the time they come into hard antler when they push and shove to exert dominance or be playful until the breeding season's over and they drop their antlers.

• Bucks are social animals and possess a herd instinct. When they hear the sound of other deer, whether those deer are fighting or just sparring, they'll often respond to those sounds.

• Young bucks and does often will come in to watch a battle when there's a fight.

"I rattle a lot throughout the season," Steve Warner, longtime avid deer hunter, wildlife biologist and vice-president of Bushlan Camouflage, reported. "But I try to go to regions where I know the bucks will be. In the mornings, I rattle in places near thick cover where I assume the bucks

78

Steve Warner rattles thick cover areas to try and pull trophy bucks like this one from that heavy cover.

have bedded-down. I'm hoping to pull those bucks out of that cover and to within bow range. Rattling will bring big bucks out of thick cover often when nothing else will.

"At mid-day or later in the morning, I may rattle in feeding sites or along travel trails. If the bucks are up and moving and hear rattling, they'll often come to it. Later in the evening, I'll go back to the thick cover." One of the most important keys to rattling successfully when you're bowhunting is to know where the buck should be before you begin to rattle. Then you will understand from which direction to expect the buck. When you hear or see him coming, you'll have time to draw your bow.

"One of the most effective methods of rattling I use is to take the horns and rake them on a small tree," Warner reported. "Many times, raking the antlers against a tree like a buck rattling a bush will call in as many if not more deer than actually clashing the antlers together." Yet another technique Warner suggests using is to grunt while you're rattling, since bucks grunt when they fight as well as before and after they fight.

"When you're rattling deer while bowhunting, often the deer will come in on the run and may not stop," Warner explained. "Or, if they do stop, they may begin to run again before you can take the shot. One of the best tools to stop a running buck is to blow the grunt call. Most of the time when a buck comes in running to the antlers you can blow the grunt call. The buck will stop, and you can take a shot. If the buck comes in running, stops out of bow range and begins to run again close enough for you to take a shot, blow the grunt call for an opportunity to shoot.

"One of the most overlooked aspects of rattling in bucks often is camouflage. As the buck comes in quickly, he is looking right at where the sound is coming from --directly at you. If you don't blend in with your environment to keep the buck from seeing you, you won't get him in close enough to take a shot with your bow.

"When I'm rattling bucks and bowhunting, I wear Bushlan camo, including a full headnet, gloves and hat. I try and have cover in front of me to break up my silhouette even more. Then I don't waste my calling and rattling sequences because the buck spots me when he comes in to where I am."

No longer does the bowhunter have to sit in the tree and hope a deer will come in and present a shot. Using these calling aids, you can make something happen when you're in your tree stand. Often calling deer doesn't work for some bow hunters because they don't continue to call throughout the season. On any given day, some deer won't come to a call. No one knows why. On other days, deer seem to come from all directions anytime you call. No hunting aid is foolproof and produces deer every time you use it.

However, from my research, I've learned that deer calling with various types of calls consistently will produce more deer within bow range than if you don't use deer calls.

CHAPTER 9

HUNT YOUR BUCK INDIAN-STYLE

Droplets of rain still hung from the limbs of the trees because of the downpour of the night before. As a light breeze gently nudged the branches, a few droplets left the limbs and hit the ground where they splattered to bring renewed life to the forest. The fog slowly lifted from the hardwood bottom.

A six point buck inched his way out of the thicket at the edge of the hardwoods. He first looked at the rotting wood of the old tree stand hunters had used long ago. Then the buck spotted the new ladder stand that had been put up just that week. He tested the air for the scent of humans but found none. Carefully he walked into the clearing, stopping frequently to test the air and watch for danger. Thirty yards from the thicket, the buck lowered his head and fed on the white oak acorns the rain from the night before had freed from the big tree above.

Occasionally the deer looked up. Then he stopped and stared for a long time at a form he'd never seen before. But after he tested the wind, stared at the form and saw that it didn't move, he ate once more.

The buck had been feeding for about 45 minutes when he heard the muffled sound of a bow string. As the deer coiled to leap, a broadhead entered just behind the buck's third rib. After sprinting 60 yards, the buck stumbled and fell in the leaves, never to rise again. Larry Norton of Pennington, Alabama, had claimed his trophy.

Stalk hunting deer with a bow is the way of the early Americans. Indians first developed this system of hunting and were deadly effective at taking game using it. However, today because of our hurry-up society, most hunters cannot refrain from walking too fast to stalk successfully. But 31-year old Larry Norton, who was raised in the rural West/Central part of Alabama, has been stalking deer most of his life.

"From the time I was a little fellow, if I was out scouting for deer, I would try to see how close I could get to the animals before I spooked them," Norton recalls. "Even today when I'm scouting before the season,

Often when you see bucks, you can sneak in close enough to get a shot.

if I spot a deer, I attempt to stalk it to learn what the deer is feeding on and to keep my stalk hunting skills honed in preparation for bow season.''

Norton has been harvesting deer consistently with his bow for the last five years. A hunting guide at Bent Creek Lodge near Jachin, Alabama, Norton is in the woods almost daily throughout deer season. The tactics he's developed will enable you to bag more bucks with your bow.

WHY GIVE UP ON BUCKS

''The best way to learn to stalk deer with a bow is to mentally give up any possibility of having the opportunity to take a shot,'' Norton explains.

''When I first started stalking deer, I decided there was no way I could move close enough to a deer to get a shot before I spooked him. But what I tried to do was move in as close as possible to the deer before I spooked him -- just to see how close I could get to the animal.''

Norton found that by giving up the possibility of a shot, he did not feel the pressure of having to hurry to the deer. The stalk, not the shot, became the game. He also learned the slower he moved through the woods, the more likely he was to be able to take a shot at a buck.

WHERE AND WHEN TO FIND DEER TO STALK

When I asked Norton why the majority of bowhunters choose to hunt from tree stands but he prefers to stalk hunt bucks, Norton answered that, ''When I'm stalking and moving through the woods, I locate much more deer sign and learn more about the deer's movement patterns on the property I'm hunting than if I spend that same amount of time in a tree stand. Also I enjoy pitting my skills at close quarters with the whitetail. Personally I feel stalk hunting a deer with a bow is a far greater challenge than taking a deer with a bow from a tree stand.''

Because usually woods are most quiet immediately after a rain, Norton prefers to stalk deer then.

"If you can't move quietly through the leaves, you'll never be able to get close to a buck,'' Norton reports.

Clearcuts, briar thickets and other types of dense cover provide the backdrop for Norton's tactic.

"I attempt to move along the edge of the cover as close to the thick places as I can get without actually being in the thickets,'' Norton mentions. "I want to be able to see out into a hardwood area so I can spot a deer. But also I want to use that thicket as back cover. Then the deer won't see me while I'm looking for him.''

When Norton is scouting, if he spooks a deer, he goes to the site where he has seen the animal to determine what the deer has been feeding on and to try to learn why the deer has been in that area at that time of day. Once Norton observes a deer in a region, then he assumes that place may be good for stalk hunting, since deer are creatures of habit. Norton waits for a clear morning after a rainy day and then returns to that region to begin his stalk.

WHAT IS THE WALK OF THE STALKER

When Norton spots a deer at 100 yards and then moves to within 15 yards to take a shot, the way he walks in the woods is a major reason for his success.

"When you step into hardwoods, look the area over for about three to five minutes, searching for movement,'' Norton advises. "Then move 20 yards, stop, and do the same thing again.''

Foot position and balance are the keys to Norton's technique for stalking. Although most bowhunters stalk on two feet, Norton stalks on one. Every step he takes is calculated, and when and how he transfers his weight from one foot to the other foot is critical to his stalk success.

"When you take the first step, you lightly put the heel of your front foot down first,'' Norton explains. "Gently and carefully rock your front foot forward with no pressure on the sole of your foot. All your weight remains on your back foot. Your front foot is just touching the ground like a limp rag.

"I wear rubber bottom boots so I can feel any sticks or twigs under my front foot. If I feel a stick under my foot, I either move the stick slightly with my foot or reposition my foot to be sure I don't snap the twig. Your ability to feel what is under your foot before you transfer your weight will determine how much noise you make when moving through the woods."

Once Norton has his front foot on the ground, he still has all his weight on his back foot. When Norton's foot in front is firmly placed, he begins to transfer his weight from his back foot to his front foot. This slow weight transfer insures steadiness and prevents noise. When Norton has transferred all his weight from his back foot to his front foot, he lifts his foot in the back slightly off the ground, carrying all the weight of his body on his foot in front. Next, he slowly and carefully brings his back foot up, keeping it close to the ground and moving it slightly in front of his front foot. As Norton walks, he carries his entire weight on only one foot at a time.

"If I'm stalking in water, I try not to ever have a foot out of the water," Norton comments. "When I'm bringing my back foot forward in the water, I slide it gently and quietly. If you take your foot out of the water, you'll make a sound. Also the water will run off your boot and splash in the water below your boot. Too, you'll disturb the water when you begin to put your foot down again. By keeping your foot in the water and sliding it instead of pulling it up out of the water, you don't make as much noise or disturb as much water and are less likely to be detected."

If a deer spots Norton as he's taking a step, he freezes and stands on one foot as long as is required to make the deer quit watching him. By making sure that each step he takes is quiet and deliberate, Norton is much less likely to spook the deer he is stalking.

HOW TO CAMOUFLAGE YOUR STALK

Now that you know how to walk and stalk a deer, you must prepare for the hunt. This preparation also is critical to your ability to get in close enough to take a shot at a buck with a bow.

"I begin by bathing with Tink's No-Stink soap from Wellington," Norton says. "I wash my body and my clothes in this product to eliminate human odor and to put odor barriers in my clothing. Next, I use either Tink's Fox Urine or Tink's Doe Urine on my feet and on my hat to mask whatever human odor my body gives off after using an odor eliminator."

Mossy Oak Full Foliage camo is the camouflage pattern Norton chooses, and he wears a hat, gloves and mask when he is stalking deer.

"I want to be as invisible as possible," Norton emphasizes. "In the South where I hunt, there always is some type of green in the woods year round. Along the edge of thickets, you'll see greenbriar, Japanese honeysuckle and water oaks that still are holding green leaves. Even out in the hardwood bottoms, many times patches of honeysuckle, briars or other green foliage that matches the green leaves of the Mossy Oak Full Foliage camo will be present.

Using his slow moving tactic, Larry Norton walks up on bucks most hunters never see.

"Another reason I like the Full Foliage pattern is because I'm moving when I stalk. If I'm hunting in the wind, the wind will cause the leaves of the foliage to move, like I'm moving, whereas the bark of a tree can't move. Therefore, if I wear a total bark pattern camo, I believe the deer will be more likely to spot me. I'm convinced when you're stalking deer, utilizing a leaf pattern camo like Mossy Oak's Full Foliage will mean you'll be less likely to spook deer than if you wear a pattern that resembles a tree trunk."

WHEN THE STALK PROGRESSES

"If I see a deer 80- to 100-yards away, I mentally decide that 45 minutes to one hour will be required for me to get close enough to that deer to take a shot," Norton explains.

As Norton slips through the woods toward the deer, he makes mental notes of the way the deer is behaving -- whether the animal is calm, nervous, feeding or walking. He also is very conscious of the wind and only will attempt a stalk when he can move into the wind or when he has a crosswind that keeps his scent away from the deer's nose.

"A slight wind helps to cover any sound you may make," Norton reports. "Too the wind causes trees and bushes to move, which also hides my movement."

As Norton walks, he never looks down. He uses the soles of his feet as his eyes to determine what is on the ground where he's placing his boot, and he utilizes his eyes to concentrate on the animal.

By making sure each step is quiet and deliberate, a hunter is much less likely to spook the bucks he stalks.

According to Norton, "I've learned some general rules of deer behavior that aid me as I stalk. Most of the time, a deer will swish its tail back and forth before it lifts its head to look around. Generally a deer also will swish its tail back and forth before it puts its head back down to feed again. If the deer is undisturbed and not nervous, the animal usually will keep its head down feeding for at least five seconds at a time.

"When I see a deer's head go down, I start counting the seconds off. I attempt to take my steps within that five second window when the deer's head is down. Although the deer may keep its head down longer than five seconds, I never assume it will. If the deer's head is down for three seconds, and I see its tail swish, I'll stop my stalk short."

Norton uses Tink's Fox Urine as a cover-up scent. Then if the wind changes as he's stalking, he believes the fox urine will help prevent deer downwind of him from smelling him and giving the alarm snort that will spook the deer he's trying to bag.

"As you move through the woods, whenever possible, keep a big tree between you and the deer you're stalking," Norton says. "Then when a deer looks in your direction, it only will be able to spot a portion of you rather than seeing your entire outline."

Larry Norton uses Indian tactics to bag bucks like this one with his bow.

NORTON'S SECRET TO STALKING

Once you've mastered this stalk hunting tactic, you must locate an area to hunt deer utilizing this method.

"The more hunting pressure a deer feels, the more nervous the animal will be and the less likely you'll be able to stalk it," Norton reports. "That's why I try and get as far away from hunting pressure as possible. Often I'll slip out in the middle of clearcuts that only may be two or three years old and use this stalk hunting strategy. I may move deep back in the woods where most hunters won't go to get away from the pressure that makes deer nervous."

According to Norton, you even can stalk hunt deer successfully over greenfields. "If a greenfield is hunted often, the deer know where to expect the hunter -- usually in a tree stand or a shooting house. However, if you get on the side of a greenfield where the deer never have seen a hunter, you may be able to move along the edge of the woodline and stalk within bow range of the deer feeding on the greenfield. Deer on greenfields that are hunted often are oriented to look for danger coming from one particular spot. If the deer are nervous or fidgety, they constantly will be watching a tree stand or a shooting house -- expecting danger. By understanding this, you can remain on the downwind side of the field, move slowly and get in close enough to take a shot with a bow.

"This technique often is deadly after gun season has begun, and the gun hunters have started setting up on greenfields. However, if you plan to stalk a greenfield, make sure gun hunters will not be hunting this region on the day you hunt and also that everyone who hunts this area knows you will be on the edge of that greenfield. Only utilize this method of stalking on private lands where the hunting is strictly controlled."

The red man learned to stalk slowly and patiently and used however much time was required to get in close enough for a shot with his bow. If he was successful, his reward was food for his family.

Larry Norton enjoys the stalk because of the excitement and the challenge presented by his being able to move in close enough, 30 yards or less, to take a bow shot at a deer.

A Norton explains, "Stalking a deer with a bow is the most intense form of hunting for me, because all my skills as an archer and as a woodsman are tested."

CHAPTER 10

UNDERSTAND THE BODY LANGUAGE OF DEER

The arrow hit the ground with a resounding thud that echoed through the swamp. Immediately, the four point buck jumped backwards like a coiled spring released after being compressed. As quickly as the deer jumped, I pulled another arrow from my quiver and nocked it to prepare for the next shot while watching the buck's tail flagging away from me. The deer only ran about 20 yards before stopping. Since I had my arrow nocked, I could study the animal. His head was up, and he was looking around but not up into the tree where I was. As the buck studied the forest floor, he spotted the arrow sticking up in the ground with its white fletchings almost seeming to glow like neon.

The deer's head went up and down as he visually examined the arrow. He stuck his neck straight out attempting to test the wind to see if any trace of odor remained that might let him know what had caused the crashing sound under his belly.

When he could pinpoint no danger, slowly and carefully, one foot at a time, he walked back toward the arrow. Every five or six steps, he stopped to look around, stick his neck out and test the air as he continued to walk slowly and deliberately to where I was. The buck had been at 20 yards when I released the arrow. Now he stood broadside at 30 yards.

I started my draw. As the buck approached the arrow, he stretched out his neck, trying to smell the shaft without actually getting too close. Finally when he was about 5 feet from the arrow with his neck extended, I let my sight pin come to rest just behind and a little low on the buck's front shoulder. I released cleanly and saw the white fletchings fly straight for and then disappear into the side of the buck.

The deer bolted and ran for about 20 yards before vanishing into a cane thicket. I listened as he crashed through the cane. Then there was silence and next a low thud. I thought about how the deer had approached and why I had gotten a second shot.

The buck had come into the white oak acorns to feed -- very calmly and never suspecting danger. I was hunting in an area with little or no hunting pressure. This 2 1/2-year-old buck had probably never seen an archer. When I released the first arrow, the deer instinctively jumped away from it. Although I would like to say the deer jumped the string, the truth was I missed him. Because the deer had felt very little hunting pressure, he was more curious than frightened. Also since he had been calm when I shot, I assumed I might be able to get off a second shot if I missed the first one.

If you can read the body language of deer, often you can anticipate that second shot and prepare for it. Understanding a buck's body language is a critical ingredient for successful bowhunting. Knowing the emotional level of the deer will tell you if you should shoot, what shot you should take, whether or not you'll get a second shot and how much you will be able to move on your tree stand. Many times we fail to connect with bucks because we hurry our shots. However, if we analyze the body language of the deer, often we can wait for a better shot or the best shot.

THE IMPORTANCE OF KNOWING A DEER'S MOODS

In recent years, psychologists and psychiatrists have determined that certain body positions reflect the emotional moods of people. If you can read body language, you can determine what others are feeling and possibly change their moods.

For instance, if someone sits with his arms across his chest and his legs crossed and leans forward in his chair, more than likely he is nervous, feels threatened and will be very cautious about what he says. However, if he sits with his legs apart, his arms open and leans back in his chair, usually he's a very open, relaxed person who doesn't feel threatened or intimidated. By studying body language, we can learn much about the individual people we deal with daily and the same is true of deer. Deer also telegraph their moods by their body language as people do.

A misconception many deer hunters have is that certain rules always apply and specific tactics always are effective in bagging bucks. They are searching for a secret strategy to use or a magic piece of knowledge that will ensure their taking a deer on every outing. However, deer are individuals, differing in the ways they move and think. They also have different emotional levels at various times of the day. Some deer naturally are nervous and skittish, while often other deer exhibit more calm personalities. Outside forces can change the moods of deer. Deer in high pressure areas consistently will be more nervous than deer who rarely are hunted. Older age bucks and does are much more skittish than younger

When the buck starts to put his head down to feed, he will pull up his head quickly to see if any danger is present.

bucks and does. A doe with a fawn will be much more high-strung and easily excited than a barren doe. Knowing what mood the deer is in when it walks in front of you can help you learn when and how to shoot and whether or not you may get a second shot.

When a buck is alert, don't move.

NERVOUS FEEDING DEER

Because this deer probably will attempt to jump the string, you may want to shoot somewhat low on this deer, anticipating the squat. Take the first good shot you get at this deer because more than likely he will spot you before you shoot.

This buck will come in very slowly to feed -- often through a thicket. Usually he will stand in thick cover for a long time looking up at the trees and out at the forest floor before he comes in and then only will move a few yards at a time, stopping constantly to look in all directions and swishing his tail frantically as though he is swatting a swarm of flies.

If does are in the area, he'll continuously watch them to see if they exhibit any hint of danger. If they are feeding calmly, often a buck will lose some of his normal wariness and calm down. If no does are in a region, he will come very slowly into the area, turning to look at every sound. Every time a squirrel barks, a tree limb falls, or a woodpecker screams, this buck will jerk his head around. When he starts to put his head down to feed, he will pull it up quickly to see if any danger is present. Before

As long as a buck has his head down feeding, you can draw and make your shot.

he takes a step forward, usually he will look in at least three directions. If he is eating acorns or shrubs, he will take the food into his mouth quickly and then bring his head up to chew. He often will swish his tail just before he brings his head up and puts his head down. This tail wagging may be the key factor to let you know when you can stand and when you can draw.

Study the deer to make sure he telegraphs his moods with his tail. Some deer do, and some deer do not. Count the number of seconds from the time the deer puts his head down until he picks it up again, which will help you pattern the deer's movements.

Once you establish a pattern, either by his tail swish or the number of seconds his head is down, you then will know when you can stand and when you can draw because the animal's head will be down. If the deer brings his head up quickly and cocks it back to either the left or the right, there is a very good chance he is about to break to run or at least to jump backwards.

Knowing a deer's mood when it walks in front of you can help you learn when and how to shoot and whether or not you may get a second shot.

Usually if a deer becomes suspicious, he will pick his head up and back and begin to turn it in the direction he plans to run. At that moment, you must release the arrow if you are going to get a shot. Also you must understand the deer will drop down and jump in the direction in which his head is pointed. The buck's head is the steering wheel of his body. If his head is up and back to the left when you release the arrow, more than likely

The author has learned the importance of understanding a deer's body language.

he will squat and jump to the left. By anticipating this movement, you can aim a little low and to the left and bag the buck.

STOMPING DEER

If a deer comes in stomping its feet, walking stiff-legged and snorting, most of the time the animal is very nervous and may suspect danger. However, I have seen a mature buck use this posture when he sees younger bucks or another buck about his same age that he wants to run out of his area.

BUCKS IN A WARRING POSTURE

A posture to look for in a buck is the warring posture. Often this attitude of deer is seen during the rut when a buck comes in bristled-up like a dog ready to fight. The buck's hair will stand on end, making his body appear to be much larger than it is. He will walk stiff-legged and sway from side to side. His ears will be back. By watching him, you will know the buck is searching for another buck he intends to harm.

You may see this posture when you use a grunt call or rattling antlers during the rut. This deer may give you plenty of time to shoot and usually will not jump the string, because this buck has come to fight, not to flee. Changing gears from an aggressive mode to a flight mode will be difficult for this buck. Often you can aim where you want the arrow to hit and not have to anticipate the buck's jumping the string.

RUNNING-IN DEER

When bucks or does run in to an area, they are coming to that place for some reason -- to fight, to respond to distress calls or to see something they are expecting to find. If you are using a grunt call, a bleat call or rattling antlers and the deer moves in quickly, more than likely you will have to shoot fast. When the deer arrives at the spot the sound is coming from, the deer will expect to see what it has heard. If the deer doesn't observe what the sounds you have made have told the deer it will see, the animal will leave just as quickly as it has responded. As soon as you spot the deer coming, prepare to shoot. Probably when the deer gets into range, he will not remain there very long for you to shoot.

Aim low on this deer because as soon as he hears the string, he will coil or attempt to jump the string. He will be spooked when he does not see or hear what he thinks he should.

CALM DEER

This deer is the one all of us seek. It will come in looking for food, rarely looking up. These deer will move and feed slowly, keeping its head down for a long time, even if it hears you move.

Also this deer is very forgiving. If you miss a shot, most of the time a calm deer will give you a second shot. You will have plenty of time to draw on this kind of deer and often can wait for the best shot. This animal is not one that forces you to rush your shot. Usually a deer will exhibit this type of behavior at the first of the season in thick cover or in areas well away from hunting pressure. A deer demonstrating behavior like this feels safe and secure in the region where you find him. You can locate calm bucks even in high pressure areas if you hunt in places where no other hunter has been. Take your time when hunting this deer. Wait on your best shot, and do not expect the deer to jump the string. Since this deer is in a calm mood and not expecting danger, more time will be required for him to shift gears from being calm to fleeing, and he will be less likely to jump the string.

ADVANTAGES OF UNDERSTANDING A DEER'S BODY LANGUAGE

Reading a deer's body language will tell you when to draw, where to aim and what to anticipate will happen when you release the arrow. The deer's body language also will tell you what type of shot to expect.

More deer are bagged with bows and arrows by those who take the time to assess the deer's mood and read the deer's body language than by those who disregard what the animal is expressing or what behavior the animal is demonstrating as he comes in for the shot. Learn to read body language and to anticipate the deer's movement. You will shoot more accurately, bag more bucks and go home with more trophies.

CHAPTER 11

USE A MASTER'S SECRETS TO BAG BUCKS

John Demp Grace was almost ready to give up deer hunting. "I had been taking deer with a gun since I was 10-years old," Grace reports. "I had bagged well over 200 whitetails, and the sport was gone from deer hunting for me."

In Grace's home state of Alabama, gun hunters can harvest a deer a day from November 20 until January 31 and two deer a day during the two-week Christmas holiday season. Because bowhunters can begin bagging a deer a day on October 15 each year, Grace's record of taking 200 deer in 30 years is not that exceptional. When you also add in the factor that Grace lives in Sumter County, one of the most deer-rich parts of Alabama, perhaps you can understand why Grace was burned out on gun hunting deer.

"But when I picked up a bow somewhat over a decade ago and hunted deer with a bow, I felt as though I was deer hunting for the first time," Grace remembers. "The sport was new, different and fresh. I had to learn how to hunt as a bowhunter, instead of a gun hunter, which meant I had to understand more about the whitetail and its habits. I had to be much closer to the animal to take a shot, and I had to become familiar with an all-new weapon."

The thrill of bagging deer with a bow was so overpowering Grace did arrow a few unantlered deer in the beginning of his bowhunting career. However, in the 1986 deer season, Grace had bagged 10-buck deer during the first six weeks of the bow season. Eighty-five percent of Grace's deer have been bagged on public lands in Alabama, and about 85 percent of the deer he's arrowed have been bucks. "I decided the real challenge in bowhunting is to take a buck deer," Grace explains. "On areas I hunted, I could harvest numerous, unantlered deer. But bagging a buck was the real sport of bowhunting for me, and the aspect of the sport on which I concentrated."

To bag a buck like this one, learn the secrets of masters.

As a hunting guide at Bent Creek Lodge in Jachin, Alabama, Grace has plenty of opportunity to bag unantlered deer as well as antlered deer. Although he does take a few deer off the more than 20,000 acres of prime hunting habitat the lodge controls, he hunts public lands on his off days. I asked Grace how a bowhunter can become a buck hunter.

SCOUT FOR BUCKS

Grace scouts for deer much like most other bowhunters. He tries to locate feeding areas, bedding regions and travel trails. However, Grace adds one other criteria to his inspection list before he decides where to put up his tree stand.

"I won't place a stand in an area if I don't see buck signs," Grace says. "Even when the whitetails aren't in rut, some kind of scrape or rub will be in a region, if the buck is using the particular spot in the woods

Often you'll have a difficult time choosing which is the trophy deer when bucks are running together.

where I choose to set up my tree stand. At the very beginning of hunting season, bucks will rub their antlers to get the velvet off. Therefore I often don't hunt spots most bowhunters will. If I come into a place with plenty of droppings, trails, cracked acorns where the deer have been feeding and disturbed leaves where the deer have stuck their noses under the leaves to pick up acorns, I still won't hunt that site if there are no buck signs.''

LET THE DOES GO

Once Grace finds a buck hotspot, he spends plenty of time in that area.

''If you're going to take a buck, you must be willing to let the does go,'' Grace comments. ''You must allow does and oftentimes large numbers of does to pass within easy bow range if you are going to take the buck deer you came to bag. This ability to pass up the does is where many bowhunters fall short of taking bucks. If a bowhunter goes ahead and yields to the temptation of arrowing a doe, and a buck is following those does, then he has spooked the male deer. More than likely he won't get a shot at the buck.

''Bucks, especially trophy bucks, are not stupid. They will run a string of decoy does out in front of them to make sure an area is safe. If the decoy doe gets arrowed, then the buck is not about to come into that same spot and have the identical thing happen to him. The first morning of one bow season, I let 12 does walk within 5 yards of my tree stand. The

99

According to John Demp Grace, "I hunt escape routes leading into or out of thick cover to bag bucks with my bow."

13th deer to pass by my stand was a spike. He was about 20 yards from the stand when I took him."

Patience, conviction and resolve are all required to sit quietly on a tree stand and watch whitetails you know you can arrow walk into and out of range. However, holding your shot is required if you are going to be a buck hunter.

TAKE THE TROPHY

Late in the season after Grace has arrowed several bucks, he becomes a trophy-only bowhunter. No longer merely satisfied with harvesting an antlered deer, Grace hunts for a trophy deer.

To take a trophy buck with a bow, "The hunter must pass up the smaller bucks," Grace observes. "The biggest buck I ever have bagged with a bow was a 185-pound, 12 point in 1983."

On this Thanksgiving Day in 1983, Grace ate Thanksgiving dinner with his mother and father but was restless. He had located a hot scrape and anxiously wanted to get into the woods to attempt to bag another buck with his bow.

"I went outside after lunch," Grace recalls. "A breeze was blowing. I realized from the direction of the wind that the wind would be right to keep my scent from being blown into the area I wanted to hunt. Since I was itching to hunt, I asked my parents to excuse me. By 3:00 p.m. I was in my tree stand.

"I was hunting a scrape under a beech tree on the edge of a clearcut that was six years old where briars and honeysuckle for the deer to feed on and bed in were abundant. At 3:20 p.m., I saw a nose and antlers in the limbs of the beech tree where the scrape was located. I was on a stand 20 yards below the scrape.

"Although the first deer coming to the scrape was a six point, I spotted two more bucks behind him. The last buck had what appeared to be a monster-sized rack. I let the six point pass. Next the eight point came in and moved to within 30 yards of my stand before turning to the right. The eight point would have been an easy and sure target, but I was hunting for the trophy.

"I watched the larger buck. Every time a dog barked, a squirrel chattered, or the wind changed, the older buck brought his head up quickly and looked in all directions. I had noticed exactly where the eight point had turned when he was 30 yards away from me. I assumed the bigger buck would follow the same course that both the six point and the eight point had taken.

"As I had anticipated, the big 12-point buck came down the path the other two bucks had traveled. He stopped and turned broadside to me at 30 yards. Normally I don't like to take a 30 yard shot, because most of the time I can get closer to a buck than 30 yards. But I knew if I was going to bag this particular deer, I would have to make the shot."

After taking the trophy 12-point, Grace never returned to that same spot to take the two smaller bucks, because, "I'm convinced I can hunt somewhere else and possibly take a bigger buck."

If you are planning to arrow a trophy buck, at times you may have to let very nice bucks walk by.

HUNT SCRAPES DURING THE RUT

Late in the season, Grace hunts scrapes as most bowhunters do.

"But I never hunt a scrape if the wind is not in my favor," Grace mentions. "I want the wind blowing into my face and not carrying my scent into the scrape. I must be able to approach the scrape from downwind, which is another important key to successful hunting that sportsmen often overlook. The approach you make to the scrape is just as critical as where you set up to try and take the deer. Besides coming to the scrape from downwind, I sneak up to the scrape as though I think a buck is watching me. I don't use any scent disguises or attractants, because I believe that no scent is the best scent for a bowhunter.

101

If you're going to take a buck, you must be willing to let the does go.

"I set my tree stand 20 yards below a scrape. Most of the time a buck will walk 10 yards below his scrape and test the air to see if there is a doe close by. Since a buck always circles his scrape, if he walks in 10 to 20 yards below the scrape, he will be within easy bow range for me. The closest I ever have taken a buck to my stand was when the deer was one step from the tree. I had to shoot straight down on him.

"Yet another critical key to successful scrape hunting is to be high up in a tree. Whenever possible, I set my tree stand at least 20 feet up in a tree. Then the deer is not as likely to look that high up and spot me. Also my scent is higher off of the ground and will be carried away further. The deer is less likely to smell me. An advantage to being this high in a tree is you rarely will shoot under a whitetail. Usually if a hunter misses, he has shot over the deer.

"Something else I have learned about shooting my bow from this high in the tree is that the deer often will be able to hear the arrow coming and may jump the string. I set my pinsight low. When I am practice shooting, I prefer my arrow to hit 4 inches low at 20 yards. Then if a deer attempts to jump the string when it hears the arrow as it usually does, I will center the lungs if I'm aiming for the heart. If the animal doesn't try to jump, I still will hit a heart shot. My aiming point is the center of the deer right behind the front shoulders."

USE A SILENT TREE STAND

Although Grace wears full camouflage, he never camouflages his face or hands, because he does not anticipate a deer's spotting him in a tree. "Most of the time when a deer sees the hunter in a tree, the tree stand probably has made some type of noise to alert the animal," Grace says. "Therefore, I use the quietest tree stand I can find and screw-in tree steps which make no noise when they are being put up. With this combination of tree steps and tree stand and by taking my time when I climb the tree, I seldom spook a deer.

"I have set up my tree stand before and sat there for an hour before a buck got up from his bed 60-yards away. Since I knew the buck didn't come in to bed down while I was in the stand, apparently he was there when I put my tree stand up but never heard me. To hunt a buck with a bow and arrows, you must be quiet and not create any noise while walking to your stand, when you are putting up your tree stand or getting into your stand."

TALK TO YOURSELF MENTALLY

Finding a place to take a buck is the first requirement for Grace's successful buck hunting tactic. Being quiet and positioning your tree stand in the best place is the second factor in successful bowhunting. However, shooting accurately when the shot presents itself will make or break a bowhunter. Grace talks to himself mentally when the buck is in front of him.

"The first thing I say to myself is, 'Pick a good shot.' I calculate the distance to the deer, let the deer present the best shot he will, look for the spot on the deer you want to shoot at, don't watch the whole deer and try to be comfortable when you have the arrow drawn back.

"Next I tell myself to, 'Have good form.' I must be certain that when I have the bow at full draw, I mentally check my anchor point, my sighting point and every other aspect of good form in archery whether I'm shooting at a deer or a target. Unless I mentally check out my form, I realize I will shoot inaccurately.

"Then I remind myself to, 'Get a good release.' Although I use a mechanical release, I want to make sure the release is smooth and not jerky -- which can throw the arrow off target. I hold my pin on the target I'm shooting, squeeze the trigger and continue to look at my sight on the spot I am shooting until the arrow hits the deer. I have found that follow-through is critical in accurate shooting. If you're not looking at the spot you're shooting until the arrow hits, you probably won't shoot as correctly.

If you are planning to arrow a trophy buck, at times you may have to let very nice bucks walk by.

"At the same time I'm squeezing the trigger, I'm saying to myself, 'I've got to have that buck. That deer must belong to me.' I never question about whether or not I'll take him. I tell myself I will bag the deer, which I believe enables me to bag more bucks."

TRAIL THE ARROWED DEER

Grace watches the arrow all the way to the deer to try and see where he hits the animal. Then he notes the reaction of the animal and the direction the deer is traveling.

"Before I leave my tree, I take a compass reading on the direction the deer is moving when I last see him," Grace explains. "I shoot an arrow with white feathers so I can see easily where I've hit the deer. Also if the arrow passes all the way through the deer, the white feathers will make reading the blood much easier than darker colored feathers.

"I always keep a practice arrow in my quiver. Then before I climb down from the tree, I shoot a second arrow at the exact spot where I've hit the buck if the arrow stays with the buck. Although most of the time the arrow will pass through the deer, to recover the animal I need to know where to start my trailing and tracking. I rarely lose an arrowed deer, because I take a compass reading on the direction the buck has fled, and I shoot a practice arrow to mark the spot where I should begin my search.

A critical key to successful scrape hunting during the rut is to be high up in a tree.

"If I hear the deer fall, I usually will come down out of the tree, go read the sign and try and find the deer. If I don't hear the deer fall, I will wait about 15 minutes before I climb down the tree and read the arrow. If stomach content is on the arrow, which will lead me to believe I may have gut shot the deer, I don't even look for him at this point. I go home, eat supper and maybe watch the news on television. Then I get my Coleman lantern and return to the spot where I've shot the deer.

"Using the lantern, I blood trail the deer. The Coleman lantern puts off a very bright, white light that makes the blood glow when the light hits it, which actually makes trailing at night much easier than in the daytime. Not putting any pressure on the deer after the shot by trying to find him keeps the deer from moving too far before he lies down. I feel very confident of my ability to find a deer after dark, therefore, I won't hesitate to take a shot late in the afternoon. If I hit the deer hard enough to put him down, I will locate him at night with a light."

PRACTICE TO BE SUCCESSFUL

Grace believes that to consistently bag deer with a bow, the hunter must know his bow better than his best friend.

"You have to be able to use one pin to shoot accurately at any distance. Even though you may have three or four pins on your bow, you must judge distance correctly and shoot straight and accurately from all kinds of positions even using one pin. I utilize a lighted pinsight for late afternoon shooting. With just one pin lit, I can shoot accurately. To become a good bowhunter, you must be a good archer. I believe that there are no shortcuts to gain proficiency as an archer.

"I recommend you join a local bowhunting club and learn to shoot targets, judge distance, improve your form and shoot at every opportunity. All the hunting skills in the world will not produce a buck if you can't arrow a deer properly when he presents a shot. Having confidence in your own ability to place the arrow in the spot you choose when you are prepared to shoot can mean the difference in consistently taking deer or missing more deer than you arrow."

John Grace has refined the sport of bowhunting to concentrate on taking bucks. He yearly bags trophies. His tactics will make us all better buck hunters with our bows.

CHAPTER 12

BOWHUNT THE BUCKS OF GUN SEASON

"I usually take my biggest bucks with a bow during gun/deer season on public lands," John Demp Grace told me several years ago.

His was the strangest comment I ever had heard an archer make, because most bowhunters I knew primarily hunted with a bow during bow season. Then when gun season arrived, they forgot their bows and picked up their 30/06s or their 7mms.

The archers of my acquaintance who continued to hunt during gun/deer season usually sought out private lands where deer were undisturbed and easier to pattern. I knew of no one who deliberately hunted high pressure public lands during gun/deer season with a bow.

JOHN DEMP GRACE

Grace bowhunts public lands during gun/deer season because, "Gun/deer season is the easiest time to find and take a big buck, especially in high pressure areas like public lands. Because gun hunters and bowhunters hunt differently, the gun hunter will force a buck to move to a spot where I can locate him easily and then bag him."

Grace explains that gun hunters most often hunt open places where they can see for 50 to 200 yards since they want to be able to spot and take deer to the maximum effectiveness of their shooting skills and their rifles' ranges. "They believe the more land they can watch, the greater their odds are for seeing a buck. Because these open places are where gun hunters walk, stalk and put their tree stands, older age class bucks have learned to avoid those areas to survive."

Grace mentions the only regions where bucks can be by the end of gun/deer season on public lands are in thick cover where the hunter can see only 30 yards or less, which are ideal stand sites for the bowhunter who wants his shot at 30 yards or less. Grace has found that older age class bucks use well-defined routes to go into sanctuary areas. By taking a stand along these routes, he consistently can bag the bucks the gun hunters drive to him.

In the first rays of light, the gun hunters will push deer into thick cover regions where the bowhunters can wait to bag the deer.

"Because deer realize which natural barriers hunters won't cross such as creeks, thick cover and property lines, the three best places for me to take a stand are at creek crossings, in thick cover or along the edges of property lines," Grace reported. "Where private land touches public land, the deer on the public land know if they can get to the sanctuary of the private land, they can avoid hunting pressure. By taking a stand on a trail that leads to private land, I greatly increase my odds for bagging a buck, especially if this private land is not hunted or is hunted very little."

Grace also has studied hunter movement patterns. He knows when he's most likely to spot bucks in these stand sites he's chosen.

"A primary time to see and bag bucks with a bow is between 9 and 10 a.m.," Grace said. "After entering the woods at daylight, most gun/deer hunters will not spend more than two or three hours on their stands before they'll feel the need to move. When the hunters climb down from their stands and start to walk around, then they will drive the bucks to me."

One of the thick places where deer often will hole up to avoid hunting pressure is in pine thickets that are 10- to 15-years old. Gun hunters rarely go into these thickets because they contain little food for deer to eat, and the trees are too small to put up a tree stand. Your only possible shot will be at a deer that jumps and runs when he sees you approach.

But, according to Grace, "The bucks are in pine thickets. I can hunt them best from a portable, fully camouflaged ground blind I make that I

Dr. Robert Sheppard hunts thick cover areas with his bow during gun season to bag bucks.

can get inside of and shoot through. A ground blind allows me to hunt anywhere I want to -- even if no tree is there for me to put up a tree stand. This ground blind is also effective in young clearcuts with no trees but plenty of deer because the region is so thickly grown-up.''

When Grace hunts creek crossings where older age class bucks will cross creeks to reach sanctuary areas most hunters won't wade, he takes a stand where he can watch both sides of the creek crossing. Then he can bag bucks coming from either direction.

''One of the nicest eight points I ever bagged with my bow was one I found early in the morning at a small creek crossing,'' Grace recalled. ''I could hear the car doors of hunters slamming off in the distance just at first light as I saw the buck approach. Just after he crossed the creek, I

One of the places where deer often will hole up to avoid hunting pressure is pine thickets 10 to 15 years old.

loosed my arrow and took him. I was on the way out of the woods before many gun hunters even reached their stands.''

DR. ROBERT SHEPPARD

Although Grace uses gun hunters to drive bucks to his stand site, Dr. Robert Sheppard, an expert woodsman and longtime bowhunter, allows gun hunters to force trophy bucks to remain in an area where he can take them at the end of the season.

''The more hunting pressure a region receives, the more time the older age class bucks are forced to spend in thick cover so they can survive,'' Dr. Sheppard explained. ''Although identifying where the trophy bucks will be toward the end of gun season is not too difficult through using maps and aerial photos, you must lay your game plan during the summer months, if you plan to take one of these bucks with a bow.''

Sheppard and Grace both are masters at scouting who spend more time scouting than hunting. However, they don't spend much time scouting during bow season or gun/deer season. Most of their scouting is done prior to the season. On new lands, much of their scouting is done with the aid of aerial photos and topographical maps of the land they plan to hunt. ''On most aerial photos, you can see thick cover areas where bucks must hide from hunting pressure,'' Sheppard said. ''You'll also spot the roads hunters use to go in and out of the woods. Once you determine the direction hunters will come from on the roads and where the thick cover areas are, then you'll know where to go to build your late season bow stand."

Sheppard goes to thick cover areas on the land he hunts during the summer months and moves 30 to 40 yards inside a thicket. "I cut a small trail to the spot in the thicket I want to hunt. Usually the trail will be no more than two feet wide -- just wide enough for me to walk without my clothes touching bushes and brambles on either side. Then I don't leave very much odor on bushes and trees as I walk. At the end of the trail in the middle of the thicket, I look for a tree to place a tree stand in or a high point to setup a ground blind. When I locate the site I'm searching for in the summer, I set up my tree stand or build a ground blind, usually facing Northwest, since the wind in Southwest Alabama where I generally hunt blows from the Northwest. I use my compass to set up my stand facing Northwest to increase my odds of having a favorable wind on the day I want to hunt."

After Sheppard selects his stand site in the summer, he then cuts four shooting lanes in the heart of the thick cover. These lanes will be three to four feet wide and will spoke out in three directions from his stand site. By having shooting lanes, he has a clear path for his arrow to fly when he sees a buck in that thick cover.

"I may return to this region just before bow season to make sure I don't have to do any more cutting or cleaning of my shooting lanes," Sheppard mentioned. "On my way out of the thicket, I will place two Bright Eyes, which are thumb tacks tipped with fluorescent paint, in trees or bushes about 8 to 10 inches off the ground where I can see them before daylight. I put them close to the ground so anyone else who spots them will think they're rabbits' eyes and not trail markers.

"If you want to take a trophy buck with your bow in thick cover during gun/deer season, you must be sure no one else hunts your stand site except you. Only by camouflaging the way you go into and leave that thicket can you be certain no one else hunts your late season hotspot." Even with time invested in preparing a thick cover hotspot to hunt, Sheppard only may go into this site once or twice during hunting season.

"I won't hunt my thick cover hotspot until the last week of gun/deer season," Sheppard explained. "The biggest and smartest bucks have felt hunting pressure all year long. The only way they've survived is by remaining in that thick cover.

"Also I only go into this site when I have a favorable wind. If I move into that thick cover sanctuary with the wind at my back, and a trophy buck

Ronnie Groom uses human odor to funnel deer off some trails and onto the trail where he has taken a stand.

smells me in his sanctuary, he'll leave, and I'll never see him. I had rather not hunt one of these sanctuary areas, even though I've spent the time and energy to cut a trail, build my stand and make shooting lanes, than hunt this spot when the buck can smell me."

On the last week of gun/deer season when Sheppard goes to his big buck site, he plans to stay in his stand all day long.

"Although big bucks won't move outside of thick cover during daylight hours in gun/deer season, they will move around in that thick cover," Sheppard mentions. "They'll stretch, walk, feed, chase does and breed in these regions. If I stay all day long, the odds are extremely good that I'll not only see but also get a shot at a very nice buck with my bow."

RONNIE GROOM

Another hunter who has learned to use hunting pressure to funnel deer to his bow stand during gun/deer season is Ronnie Groom of Panama City, Florida, a bowhunting instructor who has taken more than 100 deer.

"I believe human odor can be used to make older age class bucks go where you want them to and do what you want them to do. If, for instance, I want to hunt one side of a hill or a mountain, I will come in to my stand from the other side of the mountain, walk almost to the top of the mountain about 50 yards from my stand and walk the edge of the mountain until I reach my stand. Then any bucks coming down the side of the mountain or through the bottom where I'm not hunting will smell my odor and go to the top of the mountain where I've left no odor, walk the ridge or the other side of the mountain and come to where I'm waiting."

Groom also utilizes human odor in high pressure hunting areas, especially during gun/deer season, to funnel deer off one trail and onto the trail he's hunting.

"If three or four trails come to a food tree, then often I'll have a difficult time deciding where to put my tree stand," Groom commented. "However, I've learned if I walk across the three trails I don't want the deer to travel and only leave one trail free of human odor, most of the time I can funnel the deer from the other trails onto the trail I'm hunting."

Another tactic Groom employs when hunting trails that run through open regions is to hang a shirt or a hat just over a trail. Then a deer will see the clothing when it comes down the trail.

"Most times when a deer spots a shirt or a hat hanging over the trail, they will veer off and use another trail to come to me," Groom mentioned. "By using human odor or clothing to cancel out the trails you don't want deer to travel, you can increase the number of deer that move down the trail you're hunting. The more hunting activity you have in the area you hunt, the better this strategy will work."

One of the reasons archers lay down their bows and pick up their guns during gun/deer season is they believe guns drastically improve their chances for bagging trophy bucks or any buck. However, if you employ the strategies of John Demp Grace, Dr. Robert Sheppard and Ronnie Groom, you may find you'll not only increase your odds of bagging a buck, but also increase your chances for taking a trophy buck. These archers have learned to use gun hunters to enhance their bowhunting opportunities and to bag more deer. You can employ these same tactics to take more bucks this season.

HOW TO USE MAPS TO LOCATE BUCKS
DURING GUN/DEER SEASON

From WMA maps obtained from your state wildlife agency, you can learn where public land borders private land. Then using an aerial photo, you can see thick cover areas and creek crossings to plan your strategy for bowhunting during gun/deer season.

Also by using a topo map, you can identify saddles and mountains where deer will cross mountains to avoid hunting pressure. The trails through these saddles are often narrow and usually are ideal spots for the bowhunter to set up a tree stand during gun/deer season.

To obtain maps that will help you hunt more effectively, contact these sources: the U.S. Geological Survey, Federal Center, Building 41, P.O. Box 25286, Denver, CO 80225 for maps of states West of the Mississippi River, the U.S. Geological Survey, 1200 South Eads Street, Arlington, VA 22202 for maps of states East of the Mississippi River and the Office of Public Affairs of the Forest Service, Department of Agriculture, South Building, Room 3008, Washington, D.C. 20250 for the locations and addresses of the national forests and grasslands, each of which will have maps of those regions.

If you know where the thick cover areas are that deer must frequent to avoid hunting pressure, you too can bag bucks with your bow during gun/deer season.

CHAPTER 13

KNOW NUTS TO TAKE BUCKS

I still could feel my morning coffee warming my stomach as I looked at the thicket and watched the small, narrow trail that led to the white oak tree 20 yards in front of me. The night had been dark with only a rim of the moon visible. The woods with their Spanish moss dangling from the trees had a macabre look that reminded me of the movie from my boyhood, "The Creature From the Black Lagoon."

I had come to my stand under the cover of darkness and taken much longer than usual to put the bolts in the holes I had pre-drilled in the tree the week before. Carefully and quietly I climbed the tree, got into my stand, nocked an arrow and waited on daylight.

A certain confidence comes with knowing you have done everything right to give yourself an opportunity to take a shot at a buck with your bow. Today I had that feeling. I knew the deer were feeding on this white oak tree, which traditionally had been a hotspot for deer, since the nuts just had started falling two days before from this tree. I had remained well away from the tree when I scouted it. When I hung my tree stand, I saw where deer had been using their noses to funnel under the leaves to search for acorns. A well-worn path from the thick cover came to the tree on the edge of the clearcut. Everything I understood about deer hunting told me this spot should produce a buck.

With the first warm glow of sunlight, I saw a dark nose, a black eye and an ivory prong protruding from the thicket. Although the deer only was a four point, I would take him if he presented a shot.

When the deer looked away from me, I stood in my stand, checked my arrow and made ready to draw. While the deer inched his way out of the thicket, I studied the distance. The buck was at about 25 yards. Although he was walking toward me, quartering slightly, I made the decision that I would release the arrow as soon as he stopped. Often I had missed deer that were too close to me rather than deer that were too far away.

Finally the buck halted, bent his nose forward and began to sniff for acorns. I drew my bow and put the second pin on my sights immediately

Larry Norton studies nuts to find bucks.

behind the deer's front shoulder. When the pin stopped and rested on the very small spot I had chosen as my target, I released the arrow and heard that whopping sound all bowhunters immediately identify as a solid hit. The buck wheeled and headed back into thick cover. I heard him scrambling through the bushes, a thudding sound and then silence. I waited patiently for 20 minutes by my watch before I went to claim my trophy.

Because of the success of that first hunt, I've been nuts for bucks ever since. If you know how to hunt nut trees, you consistently can pattern and take deer year after year in the same area.

A man who has far more knowledge than myself and spends most of his time in the woods hunting nuts is Larry Norton of Pennington, Alabama, a member of Wellington Outdoors' and Mossy Oak's pro staff teams and a hunting guide at Bent Creek Lodge.

"I have several nut trees around which I usually bag a deer and often a buck each year with my bow," Larry Norton says.

Norton has developed several systems of hunting nut trees that produce deer for him each season. Using his techniques will help you arrow more bucks.

FOLLOW THE SQUIRRELS TO FIND
THE BUCKS

Both squirrels and deer feed on nut trees. By noticing which trees the squirrels are feeding on each week of deer season, you often can find deer under those same trees. In Norton's home state of Alabama, red oaks and water oaks drop their acorns first for the deer and squirrels to eat. Then the white oaks lose their nuts, and finally the large white oaks known as chestnut oaks drop their acorns. However, water oak acorns continue to fall throughout deer season and on until the end of February.

KEEP A TREE LOG

To concentrate deer close enough for a bow shot, find the first tree of each species to drop its nuts. Deer often will come from a great distance to taste the first nuts of a type of tree. Not only will squirrels tell you which trees drop their nuts first, but they also will knock nuts loose from the trees as they bounce around in the limbs, which helps put more nuts on the ground for the deer. Once Norton pinpoints the first nut tree of each kind in an area to drop its nuts, he records its location and the date in a log book.

According to Norton, "One of the most critical keys to hunting nut trees is to know when to leave one type of nut tree and when to start hunting another kind of nut tree. I have discovered the white oaks in my area usually begin dropping their nuts around the first of November, which is about two weeks after the beginning of bow season and four to six weeks

117

If you pattern the trees in your hunting area and keep a log on them, you also can pattern the deer and predict where and when you can expect to find a buck.

after the red oaks and water oaks start to drop their nuts. When the white oaks turn loose of their nuts, I can hunt successfully around a white oak tree for five to six days.

"Most of the white oak nuts will fall off a tree within a day or two, remaining on the ground for only five to seven days before the deer eat them up. If a rain occurs during the time when the acorns are on the ground, the white oak acorn will sour and rot. A white oak tree can concentrate deer and cause them to leave the red oak and water oak acorns, which are more abundant than the white oak acorns, since the deer only have a short time to feed on these particularly sweet nuts. Deer remind me of children at a picnic. Even though they may have all the food they want to eat, when the popsicle man comes around, they'll leave that abundance of food to get the sweet treat that only is available for a short time."

After hunting the white oak trees, Norton then hunts around chestnut oaks.

"The chestnut oak acorn is sweet like the white oak but is a larger acorn," Norton reports. "Deer don't have to eat as many of them as they do the water oak and red oak acorns to be satisfied. The chestnut oak seems to provide a banquet feast for the deer, whereas the water oak and the red oak are more like hors d'oeuvres."

The food supply of the chestnut oak only lasts from five to seven days -- like the smaller white oak. If you can hunt around chestnut oaks during the time the nuts are on the ground, you drastically increase your odds for taking a whitetail.

Norton has learned the chestnut oak and the smaller white oak concentrate deer better than either the red oak or the water oak. By keeping a log of the location of the trees and what date each tree drops its nuts, every year Norton accurately can predict which white oak or chestnut oak trees he should hunt around each week of bow season. Although not all trees bear nuts each season, Norton has enough trees in his log to always have a tree around which to hunt.

"An important key to remember and note in your log is that not all white oaks or chestnut oaks drop their nuts on the same day or even during the same week or the same month," Norton mentions. "If you pattern the trees in your hunting area and keep a log on them, you also can pattern deer and predict where and when you can expect to find the bucks."

After the white oaks and the chestnut oaks have stopped producing nuts, Norton once again begins to hunt water oak acorns. Norton also hunts shrubs like blackberry bushes and greenbriar (smilax) later in the season, especially if he has fertilized these plants before the season.

FERTILIZE NUT TREES AND SHRUBS

Norton has learned a secret that allows him to concentrate deer under one particular tree in an area with a large number of acorn trees in it. Often too many available acorn trees can be more difficult for the bowhunter to hunt around than when no acorn trees at all are present. For instance, if you are hunting a region with 20- to 50-white oak trees and all these trees are dropping their nuts at about the same time, deer will meander through this area feeding on nuts from all the trees, which makes getting a buck to within bow range difficult.

"I will pick one tree in a section and fertilize only that tree," Norton says. "The fertilizer makes the tree bear more nuts that also are bigger and sweeter than the nuts from an unfertilized tree. Even if you're in an area where several trees are dropping their acorns at the same time, you can concentrate the deer under the tree that has been fertilized."

Norton has a formula for selecting the trees he fertilizes.

"I first look for thick cover bedding areas deer will be utilizing," Norton emphasizes. "Then I choose the nut tree closest to the bedding region, which usually will be the first tree the deer will feed on when they

119

By buddy hunting, you both will have the opportunity to take more bucks.

come from bedding and the last tree they will feed on when they are moving to their bedding site. I generally fertilize one tree for each week of the season I plan to hunt. In other words, once I know which tree will be dropping its nuts first in that section of the woods during the season, that tree is the one I will fertilize. Then I continuously will have a newly fertilized tree to hunt next to each week of the season.

"I also fertilize trees according to species. I fertilize some water oak and red oak trees for the first of the season, white oaks for the middle of the season, chestnut oaks and water oaks for the latter part of the season and the briar thickets and stands of greenbriar and honeysuckle for the end of the season. Remember, if you want to consistently take deer from the trees you fertilize, don't tell anyone which trees you have fertilized.

"I primarily fertilize trees after deer season -- usually in February and early March before turkey season begins when no one else is in the woods. Not only is this the best time to fertilize a tree but also then no else sees what you are doing.

"Start from under the outside limbs of a tree, and use a posthole digger to dig a hole 3-feet deep. Fill the hole 2-feet deep with 13/13/13 fertilizer, and put 1-foot of dirt over the top of the hole. Place your holes about 5-feet apart all the way back to within 3-feet of the base of the tree. Dig these holes on all four sides of the tree in a spoke-like diagram to carry nutrients down to the root system."

HUNT ALONE

When Norton hunts with a bow, he tries to find two acorn trees producing a good number of acorns 50 yards apart. After fertilizing both trees, he sets a tree stand between the trees to take deer that come in to either tree. Norton places his tree stand 25 yards from the bases of both trees he wants to hunt. Using this system of fertilizing and tree stand placement, Norton doubles his odds for arrowing a buck.

HUNT WITH A BUDDY

Norton mentions that, "I can take twice as many deer by being unselfish and hunting with a partner than I can if I hunt alone."

Norton will fertilize a nut tree on the edge of thick cover and take a stand 30 yards from the base of that tree on the edge of the cover. Then he can arrow a deer from his stand 30 yards to the base of the tree that has been fertilized or 30 yards on the other side of his stand down the edge of the thicket to cover 60 yards of territory from his tree stand.

"If I put a hunting companion on the other side of the fertilized tree from me, he can shoot from his tree stand 30 yards toward the fertilized tree or for 30 yards on the other side of his stand," Norton says. "Using this tactic, the two of us can cover 120 yards of territory with our bows.

"Both of us consistently will bag more deer by hunting together than either of us will take by hunting alone. When we buddy hunt, we have four sets of eyes looking for deer instead of two. We use hand signals to communicate when either of us sees a deer. Often my buddy will spot a deer I never see and never would have gotten a shot at had he not alerted me to the deer's presence. I've been buddy hunting for 15 years. I'm convinced that if more archers hunt together, they will be more successful than either archer will be by himself.

"Another advantage to using this system of buddy hunting is if a deer comes in to range but is turned wrong for you to get a good shot, many times it will present a broadside shot to your partner. Instead of your not getting a shot or being forced to take a bad shot, your partner may have a perfect shot. Also hunting with a partner means four sets of eyes can look for blood when you're blood trailing instead of two, and you'll have four arms and legs to drag deer out instead of just two."

Hunting the nuts and studying nut trees in your area will produce more deer for you in upcoming seasons. Once you begin to see the benefits of hunting fertilized nut trees, then you'll understand why fertilized nuts are best for bucks.

CHAPTER 14

WOMEN WITH BOWS

"I spotted five deer coming down the trail toward a white oak tree that was raining acorns," Regina Terrell recalled. "The first two deer were does, but the third one was a six point. I made my draw and prepared for the shot. The deer continued to walk toward me but never stopped to offer a shot.

"At the end of the parade of deer, I saw a big eight point behind the six point. But I've learned from years of hunting that once you draw on a buck, your best chance of bagging him that day is to continue to concentrate on that deer. As the two does passed my tree stand, I realized the buck wouldn't stop unless I stopped him. I tried to whistle. However, because I had a cough that morning and didn't want to spook the deer, I had a sucker in my mouth. My whistle wouldn't work. I knew if I didn't act quickly the buck would walk out of range, and I wouldn't get the shot.

"So I told that deer to, 'WHOA!' The buck froze in his tracks. I let my pinsight on my High Country bow settle just behind the buck's shoulder and concentrated on the spot I wanted to hit. When I squeezed the trigger on my mechanical release, I watched through my sight as the fletchings headed toward the deer, hit him and vanished out of sight. This buck was the first I took during the 1992 season."

Regina Terrell is one of a new breed of bowhunters whose numbers are swelling throughout the nation. Women bowhunters are one of the fastest growing segments of the shooting sports. In the past five years, the number of women who hunt nearly has doubled.

Many women bowhunters are as deadly as black widow spiders and as knowledgeable as any bowhunter who walks through the woods. They often take more deer than any of the other hunters in the bow camps where they hunt. But you won't see them in their tree stands without their lipstick and makeup.

Ellon Rutherford of Remlap, Sherry Clough of Glencoe, Kathy Caudle and Regina Terrell both of Gadsden -- all Alabamians --are four of the best women bowhunters in America today. Ranging in age from 24

Kathy Caudle knows how and where to find a buck.

to 50 years and in size from 5'2" to 5'9", these women have archery skills to rival those of Robin of Loxley, better known in English history as Robin Hood.

Because of their abilities to find and take deer and be silent in the forest, they would have eluded even the best of the Sheriff of Nottingham's soldiers. If they had lived in England during the time of Robin Hood and the outlaws of Sherwood Forest, they surely would have been a part of the legendary hero's outlaw band.

Tournament archery and bowhunting prowess go hand-in-hand. To effectively and consistently bag deer with bow and arrow, you must be able to shoot straight and take a shot under pressure -- whether in archery competition or when trying to down a wily whitetail. These four ladies have a combined experience of more than 40 years of shooting their bows and hunting. Their combined tournament archery wins include more than 12 state championships, 14 regional championships, two national titles and 3 world championships. These women not only have passed the tests for tournament archery and bowhunting deer, but their tactics can help all of us become better archers and bowhunters.

Dave Hart of Huntsville, Alabama, one of the nation's leading professional archery coaches and owner of Hart's Archery, says, "These women can shoot as well as any archer who goes into the woods to take deer. Their skills on the tournament range have proven their mastery of their equipment. Their successes in the woods have demonstrated they can hit targets. They also know how to pinpoint places to take deer, put their tree stands where they can get shots, arrow bucks, blood-trail wounded deer and bring the animals out of the woods. These ladies also have proven that neither age nor size affects their abilities to draw a bow and be successful at tournaments and in the field.''

You can learn many secrets for taking whitetails with bows from these women of the woods.

HOW TO FIND A BUCK
KATHY CAUDLE

I use a very simple step-by-step approach to finding and bagging deer. Whether or not I've ever hunted the land before, this basic formula always seems to put me in the right place at the best time to take a buck with my bow, which is the most critical key to success.

During the pre-season, I spend plenty of time looking for bucks with my binoculars. Before the season comes in and the rut starts, bucks usually will travel together. Often I will see these bucks along the edges of greenfields, around agricultural crops or in acorn flats. I like to watch the bucks before the season arrives to decide which animal I want to try and arrow during the coming season and about where I can expect to meet that buck.

Next I go into the woods and look for the trees the bucks have used to rub their antlers. These marked trees usually are easy to find and will reaffirm my assumptions that I am in a region where my odds are good for bagging a buck.

Then I search for the food sources the bucks more than likely will feed on -- acorn trees, agricultural crops or preferred shrubs and bushes. Most who bowhunt deer stop their scouting once they locate a food source. However, I've learned that even if bucks are feeding on these preferred food sources, most of the time they will use a thick cover corridor to get to that food -- a briarpatch on the edge of an agricultural field, a 3-year old clear-cut with a white oak acorn tree growing beside that clear-cut or a sage field that corners into a hardwood bottom. I search for these kinds of places to put my tree stand. Bucks, especially mature bucks, don't want to be exposed any longer than possible to open woods. They prefer to have heavy cover close to where they feed. Then if danger arises, they can retreat to that cover quickly.

Another site I like to hunt for bucks is funnel areas. When I find a narrow neck of woods between two large woodlots, I believe my chances of seeing a buck are greatly increased. Most of the deer from both large woodlots will funnel through a narrow neck rather than crossing a terrain

Regina Terrell is both a tournament archer and a master bowhunter.

break like a creek or an open field. Another advantage of hunting funnels or necked-down woods is any deer you see will be within bow range if the funnel is less than 60-yards wide and you take a stand in the middle of that funnel.

Yet another critical factor to choosing the right stand site is the direction of the sun and the wind. I prefer to have the sun at my back and the wind in my face when I'm hunting deer with a bow. If the buck comes from in front of me, he won't be able to smell me. With the sun at my back, if the deer does look up into the tree where I have my stand, he will be much less likely to see me.

Also I climb high into a tree to hunt. I like my tree stand to be at least 20 to 30 feet off the ground. At that height, I am above the buck's natural gaze -- if and when he looks up. I also can move more freely without the deer's spotting me when he comes in and presents the shot.

To be successful from a stand this high or higher in a tree, you must set your bow up to shoot from that height. Before the season when I'm practice shooting, I put my tree stand up 20 to 30 feet in a tree and shoot from that distance. The higher you climb in a tree, the smaller the kill zone of the deer becomes, because your shot will be more vertical than horizontal. When you line up your shot at a deer from this height, you must be conscious of having the arrow pass down through the heart and lung area instead of going straight through the heart and lungs as you would if you were shooting from a lower level and had a more vertical shot. To aim properly when I'm high in the tree, I aim somewhat higher on the deer than if I am shooting from 10 to 12 feet off the ground.

During the rut, I like to hunt scrapes. I prefer to hunt a region with a long scrape line rather than hunt an area with only one or two scrapes. Usually I place my tree stand near the scrape in the thickest cover. I have found these scrapes are the ones a buck will work more frequently during daylight hours, because he doesn't expose himself to the hunter nearly as much in thick cover as he will in open woods.

Bucks work scrapes when hunters can't see them at a time when the fewest hunters are in the woods. That's why I've become a bad weather bowhunter. I see and take more bucks on rainy days or snowy days when the weather is so miserable no one wants to hunt.

I'm convinced that older age class bucks understand when we hunt and don't hunt and that this knowledge dictates when they do move. I've discovered I can be the most successful taking deer with a bow on the days the weather prevents other hunters from hunting. From my in-the-woods observations, I believe bucks move longer in the mornings, come out earlier in the afternoons and move more frequently through the middles of the days when the weather is bad than they do when the weather is good.

WHEN TO TAKE THE SHOT
REGINA TERRELL

To understand when to take the shot, you must know the maximum distance at which you consistently can put your arrow in the kill zone. For most archers that's 30 yards or less. When you go into your tree stand, determine where 30 yards is from your tree stand. Look for shooting lanes where you can shoot your arrows at the deer without the shaft's hitting limbs or brush.

Determine not to take the shot unless the deer appears in the shooting lanes inside your 30-yard accuracy range. If you don't take the shot, your chances of hunting that same deer on another day still may be good. But

When Sherry Clough draws her bow, she concentrates so hard on the spot she wants to hit that she isn't conscious of releasing her arrow.

if you take the shot and miss or wound the deer, you may not have another opportunity to take the same deer from that stand site that year.

Your best chances for a clean kill are to put your arrow through both lungs or the heart of the deer. This shot will present itself when the buck either is broadside to you or quartering slightly away from you. Make the mental decision before you see the deer not to release the arrow unless the shot is presented. My aiming point is always behind the deer's front shoulder. Then my shaft will clear the shoulder blade, and the broadhead will pass through the heart/lung area.

Generally the deer I arrow are standing still with their heads down feeding. I prefer to hunt food sources. One of the keys to know when to take the shot is the deer's tail. When a buck has his head down feeding, he usually will swish his tail back and forth just before he raises his head. When he has his head up, often he will swish his tail just before he puts his head back down.

When a buck is in my accuracy zone, I'm standing and prepared to make the draw when the buck enters that 30-yard range. When the deer's head is up, I watch for him to swish his tail. When I see his tail go back and forth, I prepare to make the draw. Once the buck puts his ears back and starts to lower his head, I draw and prepare to release the arrow. If a deer brings his head up quickly when you are at full draw, lays his ears back and begins to cock his head either to the left or right, he's preparing to leave the area. The deer's head is its steering wheel. The direction in which a deer moves his head will tell you the direction in which he will run when he either smells you or has seen something that spooks him. If you're going to get a shot, you must take it at that moment. Since the deer already is alerted, you can expect him to attempt to jump the string. If a deer tries to jump the string, he's actually squatting to prepare to spring out of the area. When a deer squats at the sound of the bow, more than likely you will shoot over him. If the deer has his ears laid back and his head cocked to the side and you know he is ready to leave an area, aim for the lower part of the heart -- about two to three inches above the bottom of the chest. By using this aiming point, then if the deer does attempt to jump the string, your arrow will enter his lungs when he squats. If he doesn't squat, you will make a clean .heart shot.

HOW TO MAKE THE SHOT
SHERRY CLOUGH

When you have a big buck standing in front of you at 30 yards or less, nervousness, buck fever, anxiety, anticipation and fear all can prevent you from making an accurate shot. Only an archer who has had a big buck in his sights at close range knows the amount of pressure you can feel when you are at full draw and ready to make the shot. The way you deal with that pressure determines whether or not you will make an accurate shot and a clean kill. If you can't handle the pressure, you will miss the buck.

I've learned the best way to make a clean shot when the buck is in front of me is to not think about the shot at all. Instead, I shoot instinctively. I depend on my subconscious to cause me to shoot precisely. When I'm ready to take the shot, the deer, his antlers and his size don't exist for me. The only thing you should be thinking about is that small spot on the animal where you want to place your shot. Look for a shadow, a hair standing up or a different color of hair on the deer's side where you want to put your arrow. That spot is the only part of the deer you should be concerned with to make an accurate shot.

Once I've located where I want to shoot and am at full draw, I go through my automatic shooting sequence. I make sure my foot position is correct, I take a deep breath, and I relax. I've already made the decision that when the buck is at 20 yards, I will be aiming with my 20-yard pin. I draw the bow slowly -- all the way to my anchor point. I have my bow set up so that when I reach my anchor point, my bow is pulled as far back as it will go, which is called the back wall. I want to make sure when I get my bow fully drawn that I am pulling my bow with my back and not just with my arms and hands. Once I know I'm on the back wall of my bow, and I'm anchored correctly to make the shot, I begin concentrating on

129

looking through my peep sight and making sure my 20-yard pin is on the place I want to hit with the arrow.

I shoot a mechanical release, but I never think about squeezing the trigger when I'm ready to shoot my bow. If I do, my attention will not be on my aiming point but rather will be on the trigger. Then I've lost my concentration to do what is required to make an accurate shot.

Instead of thinking about the trigger, I focus all my energy looking at the place the deer I'm trying to hit and making sure I hold the pin on that place. I let my subconscious actually squeeze the trigger. I concentrate so hard on the spot I'm aiming for and keeping my pin on that spot that when the arrow is launched, I usually am somewhat surprised. By being relaxed, concentrating on where on the deer you're attempting to hit and not thinking about the deer or the trigger on your mechanical release, you can and will shoot more accurately.

Even when the arrow is launched, I continue to look through my peep sight at the place on the deer I want to hit. I watch the arrow strike the deer where I've aimed before I ever bring my bow down. I believe this follow-through is another critical ingredient to shooting accurately.

Whether I'm taking a shot at a trophy buck when I'm hunting or shooting the last arrow in a world class archery tournament, I relax. Daily I practice a form of relaxation exercise by sitting in a dark room at night. I close my eyes and turn off the TV or radio or anything else that may distract me. I try to get as relaxed as possible concentrate on slowing my breathing and my heart rate down. Then when I am under pressure either in a tournament or when I'm making a shot at a buck, I can take deep breaths and relax -- much like I do when I'm in my room at night. The automatic, subconscious part of my mind can go through my shooting sequence and cause me to make the shot while I focus all my attention and energy on the spot where I want to place the arrow.

HOW TO FIND THE BUCK AFTER THE SHOT
ELLON RUTHERFORD

As soon as I make the shot and see the arrow hit the deer, I pinpoint some kind of landmark -- a particular bush, tree or a large rock -- in the area, anything that will let me know where the deer was when I delivered the arrow. Once I've located a landmark, I look at my watch and make sure I stay in my tree for at least 30 minutes. I don't want to pressure the deer and cause him to run further than he normally will.

After I climb down from my tree, I search the site where the deer was when I released the arrow. If I find my arrow, I look at the color of the blood to try and determine where I have hit the animal. A very bright, pink color of blood usually indicates a lung shot. Then I'll expect to locate the

When Ellon Rutherford starts tracking deer, she usually finds her quarry.

deer quickly. If I find stomach content on the arrow, I realize the deer has been gut-shot. I may leave the woods and not return for three or four hours to be certain the deer has had plenty of time to lie down without pressure. If deep, red blood is in the area, I only may have hit a muscle and produced a flesh wound.

From the blood and the material on the arrow, I usually can determine whether to begin tracking the deer or leave the woods and begin my blood trailing at a later time. If I am confident I have a solid hit, I'll move from one spot of blood to the next on the blood trail.

I've found that one of the key ingredients to effective blood trailing is to not concentrate all my attention on the ground. A deer that is well-arrowed will leave blood on trees, bushes and grasses up off the ground. If you only watch the ground, you will see but a portion of the blood trail. To successfully recover deer, I must go where the blood trail leads me. Sometimes I'll get down on my hands and knees and crawl through briars to remain on a trail and find my deer.

When a blood trail runs out, I assume the deer has turned to the left or the right. I begin to circle the area where I've found the last traces of blood. Oftentimes I'll pick the trail back up again that I may have lost. If I fail to locate the blood trail after making several circles at the end of the trail, then I look for the thickest cover in the region, since perhaps the deer has bled out. When a buck is about to lie down, he usually will look for something to hide under or in like a blown-down tree, a ditch or a thicket.

If I don't find thick cover, then I search for the closest water. When the trail runs out, I either will pick up the trail again or the deer will be in or near water or in or under some type of brush -- usually less than 100 yards from where the trail stops. If the deer isn't within that 100 yards, then I'm fairly confident I haven't made a good hit.

I don't believe in pressuring a deer once it's hit. Many times I won't start to blood trail an animal until after dark, if I've taken a shot late in the afternoon. When I go into the woods to find the trail at night, my husband usually carries a Coleman lantern. I'll have a flashlight. The bright light of the Coleman lantern will make the blood almost glow. Blood trailing often is much easier after dark than in the daytime.

If the deer goes into a thicket, I can look into that thicket better with a flashlight than with a Coleman lantern. If I'm sure I have a good hit on the deer, generally I will locate the animal. The key to finding a deer is to walk the blood trail slowly and patiently. Don't give up until you're absolutely certain you have not inflicted a mortal wound on the deer.

These four women share ...
● a love of the solitude of a tree stand at first light,
● the excitement that comes from making a clean shot and
● the satisfaction that accompanies trailing and finding their animals and taking food home for their freezers.

The good news for women interested in archery and bowhunting is the time is always right for this sport. You're never too young or too old to shoot a bow and archery is a sport you can participate in year-round.

CHAPTER 15

RETURN OF THE LONGBOW

"I started shooting a longbow because I couldn't hit a deer with a compound," Byron Ferguson of Hartselle, Alabama, said. "Sure I could punch holes in paper targets in the backyard with a compound, but when a deer presented itself for a shot, I just couldn't hit it.

"My main problem was I couldn't judge distance accurately. I never missed a deer to the left or the right but always shot either above or under the animal. Using a longbow and shooting instinctively solved that problem for me."

Not only did Ferguson resolve his hunting dilemma, but his prowess with a longbow became so widely acclaimed, he was the first American invited to Europe to demonstrate his longbow skills since the legendary Howard Hill last toured the Continent some 40 years ago.

"Shooting instinctively with a longbow is no different from throwing a pass with a football," Ferguson explained. "In football, you mentally see the trajectory of the ball and the place where the receiver must be to catch the ball. Then you simply turn your body and throw the ball to intercept the receiver at the predetermined spot.

"Instinctive shooting with a bow is as natural, simple and quick as throwing a football. I personally believe the longbow is much faster, more accurate and better for hunting than shooting a compound bow with sights, especially when you're shooting at running game. With a compound, the draw is interrupted by the break-over of the cam. The eye must then see past the sight to pick up the image of the deer, while trying to judge the distance and attempting to calculate how much lead to use."

HOW FERGUSON WAS INTRODUCED
TO THE LONGBOW

Ferguson was introduced to the longbow by Jerry Hill, the nephew of Howard Hill, who shot the Robin Hood scenes in the Errol Flynn movie and took every type of game, including African animals with his bow in the 1920s, 30s and 40s.

"I had shot a recurve and then a compound for eight years before I began using a longbow about 10-years ago," Ferguson reported. "The first time I picked up a stick bow was awkward. However, the longbow was fun to shoot because I didn't have to worry about what might go wrong with the compound equipment to keep me from shooting accurately. I didn't have to be concerned about whether or not the bow was out of tune, whether my sight pin was slipping or not, or whether or not my mechanical release was firing correctly. All I had to do was draw and shoot.

"Because the longbow was more fun to shoot than the compound, I started shooting it more. When Jerry and I took a Frisbee and rolled it across the yard or threw it up in the air and tried to shoot it with a longbow, I really started having fun. There are now organized competitions for wing shooting with a longbow at aerial targets. Being able to hit one of those flying targets is tremendously rewarding."

In the beginning stages of Ferguson's introduction to the longbow, he'd take a compound to hunt with in the mornings and afternoons. In the middle of the day, he'd carry his longbow, because it was lighter, and practiced shooting at various non-animal targets while he scouted. One day on a scouting trip, Ferguson came up on five deer.

"I was walking down a wash when I reached a place where a log had fallen across the ditch," Ferguson remembered. "The log was between waist to shoulder-high. I bent over to go under the tree. When I looked up, I saw the deer. Since I couldn't stand up to make a normal shot, I turned my longbow parallel to the ground, drew an arrow, aimed at a spike and released. Not only did I hit the spike, but I killed him in his tracks.

"What amazed me was I was able to turn the bow, draw, aim and shoot automatically without having to go through any of the gymnastics associated with shooting a compound bow. I didn't need a mechanical release, a 50-percent let-off or the peep sights compound shooters must use to shoot accurately. From that one experience, I learned for me that the longbow was a superior weapon for taking deer."

Ferguson believes archers can do anything with the longbow they can with a compound and even more in a hunting situation.

"One of the greatest advantages to using a longbow is the hunter can shoot instinctively and get off a shot at running game quicker and better than a compound bowhunter can," Ferguson said. "If you're hunting with a compound and a deer sees you start to make your draw and bolts, more than likely you'll just let the bow back down and watch the deer run off. With a compound, you can't complete the draw, allow the bow to break over, find the sight pin, judge the distance, calculate the lead and get the shot off before the deer vanishes. However, with a longbow you just draw quickly and shoot."

The longbow with its intensive aiming requirements offers the ultimate challenge.

Byron Ferguson has proved his mastery of the longbow in the United States, Europe and Asia.

Ferguson has bagged seven running deer with his longbow and doesn't hesitate to take a shot when a deer is in range just because the animal is running. Ferguson also has found a skilled bowhunter can be much more accurate at unknown distances with a longbow than with conventional gear.

"Put yourself in this position," Ferguson suggested. "A very nice Pope and Young buck stands in front of you. Would you rather pick the spot you want to hit, and then draw and release the arrow, or would you prefer to look at that same spot, pull back a mechanical release, find the peep sight, look through the sight to find the proper sight pin to put on that spot, make sure you're holding the bow at the right angle and try and touch the mechanical release trigger at the right time when the pin you see through the peep sight is on the spot you want to hit on the deer?

"I personally believe more things can go wrong when a hunter is depending on that much equipment to make an accurate shot and on his mind to be able to judge distance accurately than if he relies solely on his eyesight and has learned to trust his instincts to shoot accurately. Because shooting instinctively means less to remember, I think a hunter is more likely to shoot accurately."

Bucks still fall to the masters of longbows as they have since the beginning of bowhunting for deer.

HOW TO GET STARTED

A disadvantage to shooting the longbow is it requires extensive practice to develop your automatic aiming systems. Ferguson is convinced all beginning bowmen should start by shooting compound bows with sights before going on to the longbow.

The compound bow with its let-off and aiming aids will allow the archer to quickly develop basic shooting skills and shoot accurately. Also the compound bow, because of its let-off, lets the hunter pull a heavy bow yet only hold a fraction of that weight.

"The compound bow helps you to develop the muscles required to shoot the longbow," Ferguson said. "A compound is also a good training aid for learning correct archery form. Because of the let-off of the compound, practicing your shooting form until it is near perfect is easier. To be accurate with a longbow, good archery form and knowing how to anchor to shoot straight and how to hold the bow and arrow correctly are essential ingredients. If you learn to shoot with good form, the accuracy will come. Once a compound bow shooter develops muscles strong

137

*When Ferguson draws his longbow, his instinctive   sighting system
allows him to shoot even dimes out of the air.*

Archers can do anything with the longbow they can with a compound and even more in a hunting situation.

enough to pull and hold a longbow, he should begin with a 45-pound longbow and work his way up to the heavier bows."

WHY SHOOT A LONGBOW

Although there are many reasons for taking up the longbow, archers who have mastered the recurve, the compound and the overdraw bow often do so because they are searching for a greater challenge. The longbow, with its instinctive aiming requirements, offers the ultimate challenge. Some longbow shooters also feel as Ferguson does about not shooting as accurately in the woods when using other equipment. To them, the longbow is a simpler, quicker, more accurate method of shooting.

Many traditionalists claim the sports of archery and bowhunting have become so mechanized they are losing their identities. These bowmen have reverted to longbows as a way to return to the purer days of the sport. To them, being able to take a deer with a longbow--the only way--is the ultimate challenge.

To become a longbow hunter, Ferguson suggests using a bow with a draw weight of at least 40 to 45 pounds. After years of experience with a longbow, Ferguson now shoots an 80- to 85-pound longbow. Howard Hill once hunted with a 100- pound bow.

The longbow arrow can be either the same aluminum shaft shot in compounds or cedar shafts. However, the arrows can't have vanes but must have feather fletchings, because the vanes will not lie down as the arrow passes across the shelf (arrow rest) as natural feathers will. Ferguson prefers using cedar shafts.

"I like the cedar arrows because they seem to recover quicker than aluminum arrows," Ferguson said. "Remember two forces are acting on the arrow simultaneously when it's released from the string. The shaft bows up from the energy released at the nock and wraps around the bow as it comes through the shelf. I personally believe the cedar shaft arrow will recover quicker from these two forces than the aluminum shaft will, which means the cedar shaft will fly straighter quicker than an aluminum shaft.

"This quick recovery is critical to accuracy when you're hunting in heavy cover. If you're hunting in a thicket and there's a small hole 10 yards out that you must shoot through to take a deer, a cedar shaft will recover quickly enough to fly straight by the time it reaches that hole."

Ferguson encourages other archers to shoot longbows because of the sheer enjoyment using this bow brings.

"Most bowhunters have much more native ability than they realize," Ferguson said. "When they take up the longbow, they are usually pleasantly surprised at how accurately they can shoot almost immediately.

"The human brain is an amazing machine that has the ability to calculate distance, arrow flight, windage, trajectory, speed of the target and the point of impact as rapidly as any computer. Using a longbow, a hunter can rediscover abilities he never realized he had. This is part of the joy of shooting a longbow. With practice, the longbow shooter will learn he is a much better archer than he ever believed he could be."

CHAPTER 16

A TRIO OF BOW-KILLED TROPHIES

What makes a trophy a trophy -- the massiveness of the antlers or the size of the deer's body? Is a trophy deer one that is as big or bigger than what an organization says a trophy animal should be, or have we begun to value the animal's size more than the experience of the hunt? Is a 12-point buck with a 22-inch beam taken by a hunter in a jeep near a feeder in Texas as much a trophy as a spike bagged by a bowhunter who must crawl 200 yards to take a shot?

Each sportsman must decide in his own heart what constitutes a trophy hunt. Each outdoorsman has that one difficult shot, that great shot or that trophy buck taken that never will be forgotten. Ronnie Groom of Panama City, Florida, Dr. Bob Sheppard of Carrollton, Alabama, and Marlowe Larson of Morgan, Utah, are all master bowhunters. Although they have harvested many deer, each of these hunters has a special hunt he remembers more than any other. Here each man recalls his trophy hunt with a bow. We'll learn that for these men, the experience made the hunt a trophy hunt, not the size of the animal bagged.

BOB SHEPPARD'S IMPOSSIBLE BUCK

Although Dr. Bob Sheppard is a cardiologist and preaches daily against smoking, drinking, overeating and other addictions that harm the human heart, Sheppard himself has one of the worst addictions I've ever witnessed. However, the good news is that Sheppard's addiction is not fatal, is very rewarding and puts food on his family's table. Sheppard is totally committed to the sport of bowhunting. In Sheppard's home state of Alabama, he begins hunting on October 15th each year and rarely misses a single day of deer hunting before the season ends on January 31st. He legally can harvest a deer a day of either sex, and during the two-week Christmas holidays, he can bag two deer a day.

Although Sheppard has taken many nice bucks with his bow, there's a spike he feels is one of his greatest trophies.

"I was hunting immediately in front of Bent Creek Hunting Lodge three years ago, when a spike and two does came into view," Sheppard remembers. "I had set my tree stand in a small neck of woods bordered by a clearcut and a point on a creek. I felt the deer would have to move through this small neck of woods to prevent entering the water or exposing themselves in the clearcut.

"When I spotted the deer, I knew I had guessed correctly and felt confident I could get a shot. But the deer turned toward the creek and were feeding about 30 yards away from me at a slow, steady pace. Because I was facing into the wind, they never smelled me. Although I knew I had plenty of time to make the shot, I'm not a long distance shooter and 30 yards was at the outer edge of my confidence level. However, I thought I could make the shot, even though it would be a long one for me.

"But I had another problem to solve. Halfway between the deer and me was a large limb that extended from an oak tree and completely covered my view of the spike's side. I realized there was absolutely no way I could shoot, because I couldn't see the target.

"Everything about the hunt had gone as I had predicted up until that time. The deer had come by my stand from the direction I thought they would come and were now within range. The direction of the wind had kept them from smelling me. My hunt plan had worked perfectly except for that one limb.

"While the deer remained in that spot for a long time, I carefully analyzed my situation. I realized the bow I was shooting was a light bow, which would cause the arrow to drop considerably at 30 yards. Even if the limb wasn't in the way, to hit the deer in the lungs, I would have to aim and shoot over the deer about 3 feet, because I only use one sight pin to aim. If my aiming point was correct, the arrow might fly over the limb, drop behind the limb, and hit the kill zone of the deer. I never had taken a blind shot like this before and never had heard of anyone else having to shoot like this. I had shot enough to know how much the arrow would drop. Even if I was wrong, the worse that could happen was that I would have to explain to my friends why there was an arrow stuck in a tree limb well off the ground.

"The light was fading as I decided to try this weird shot. I drew the bow, anchored my shot, took aim and let the arrow fly. I watched the arrow go over the limb and then vanish in less than an instant. I heard the dull thud of the arrow's hitting the deer and watched the deer run 20 yards and drop dead. I was so surprised and overwhelmed I'd made the shot that I nearly fell out of my treestand.

"This shot was the strangest and most difficult one I ever had made. I was amazed my reasoning had proven to be correct. Although the animal was only a spike, the shot itself, not the deer, made that hunt an

Often a trophy buck is more than an animal with large antlers and a heavy body weight.

extraordinary experience. A trophy is meaningful only to the one who earns it. That difficult shot made that spike one of the greatest trophies I ever have taken."

MARLOWE LARSON'S RUNNING BUCK

Marlowe Larson, who is ranked fifth in the Professional Archery Association, is one of the nation's best shooters. He hunts the wide, open land of the West, where mule deer are his primary targets. Larson is also the bow designer for the Browning Company and makes his living studying arrow flight, trajectory and all the mechanical and engineering factors that cause an arrow to fly from the string to the target in a certain amount of seconds.

Like the great baseball pitcher, Dizzy Dean, once said, "If you done it, it ain't bragging," and Marlowe Larson regularly has made phenomenal shots that now they have become almost commonplace to him. Even so, one shot will live in his heart and mind for the rest of his days.

"Before I tell my story, I think I should explain my philosophy of shooting," Larson says. "I don't believe a bowhunter should take a shot that he's not confident he can make. An iffy shot should be a no-shot. Every bowman should know his effective range and not try to exceed that range. As an archer builds experience, he can increase his range and the type of shots he can take. Here's my most unforgettable hunt.

"My brother, my two nephews and I were hunting the desert country of Utah a few years ago. In this area, we use a tactic called brushing, which easterners would call putting on a man-drive. After several days of hunting, we located in one of the draws we were hunting a large, four-point muley buck, which would be classified by easterners as an eight point, since westerners only count the points on one side of the antlers.

"This very smart buck dodged both the drivers and standers every time we tried to move him out of the draw. Although we were confident we could bag the buck, we were having a hard time determining how to get him within bow range. We've learned when hunting mule deer that if hunters don't pressure the deer constantly, the deer usually will bed down and stay in about the same area most of the time. Even though we did drive the same region a couple of times, we didn't push the deer hard enough to run him out of the draw.

"On the third day of the hunt, we methodically worked out a plan that should allow one of us a shot at the big four point. We decided all of us would make long stalks from four different directions toward the draw where we believed the buck was bedded-down. We hoped that by moving slowly and quietly, we would all get close enough to the buck that one of us would be able to get a shot when he did get up from his bed. We stressed

Dr. Robert Sheppard calculates his shot very carefully to be able to bag his buck.

safety and advised all in the party not to shoot unless the deer presented a clean shot away from the other hunters.

"We began to drive. Before I had gone only a few hundred yards, one of my nephews spooked the buck. The muley was running parallel to me at 55 yards along the top of a ridge. When I saw the deer running the ridge, I immediately pictured the image I was familiar with in tournament archery -- the running deer target.

"Often after a tournament is over, many of the contestants shoot a three dimensional deer target that is pulled at varying speeds along a track.

Each sportsman must decide in his own heart what constitutes a trophy bowhunt for him.

To hit the target, a bowman must be able to judge speed, distance and arrow flight instantly. I've always felt that shooting these moving targets helps a competition shooter to hone his skills, and besides, these running deer targets are fun to shoot.

"I realized the four pointer running the ridge was offering me a shot I consistently had made before. I quickly drew the bow, let my arrow fly and watched the arrow as the buck moved toward the shaft. The arrow drove home. Since my brother and nephews had heard the deer break from cover, they reached a vantage point where they could see what was happening. The muley, which weighed 200 pounds, fell within only a matter of seconds after the arrow hit.

"Later, my brother and his boys bragged on my lucky shot, never realizing no luck was involved. I had practiced the shot, I knew I could make the shot, and I never would have taken the shot unless I was sure of a kill. But making that shot in front of my family will be a memory that will last a long time for me."

RONNIE GROOMS' ISLAND BUCK

Ronnie Groom, a sporting goods store owner and longtime avid bowhunter who has bagged more than 100 deer with his bow, is a dedicated hunter. The ability to think like a deer, to eliminate all the reasons why a deer won't come to within range and to take advantage of the slightest mistake an animal makes to get off a shot are some of the things that make Groom one of the nation's leading bowhunters. So intent is Groom in his pursuit of whitetails that he travels three states each hunting season to bowhunt deer as much as he can.

But Groom is not just out to try to take deer. He has a much nobler calling. His mission, as he sees it, is to learn all he can about whitetail deer and then use that knowledge not only for his own sport but also to teach others in the various bowhunting schools he conducts each year. Groom's goal in bowhunting is to become the ultimate hunter. For one brief moment in time, he feels he accomplished that feat.

"I was hunting St. Vincent's Island near Apalachicola, Florida," Groom explains. "The island is unique because it is made up of a series of sloughs and ridges, which were once sandbars before the island was formed. Since I was participating in the opening morning hunt, I knew the deer would follow their normal movement patterns along the ridges. However, traditionally after the animals feel the first pulse of hunting pressure, they move to thick cover and become difficult to hunt. But on opening day, I felt I had a good chance to take a nice deer.

"I went to my stand site before daylight. The morning was quiet, dark and still. I listened intently for any deer or hunter movement, which I

147

expected to occur just at daylight. Oftentimes, when hunters enter the woods at first light, they spook deer, which in turn spook other deer.

"Thirty minutes after I reached the woods, I heard a deer running down the ridge and soon saw a big, eight-point buck. I knew I wouldn't have a chance to bag him unless he stopped. If he smelled my scent along the trail I had taken across the ridge to my stand, he might pause long enough for a shot.

"Many times when a deer first hits human scent, he will stop, look and listen to try to spot the hunter. Even though a buck is running, when he smells human odor, he often will attempt to find the hunter before he continues his flight. The animal doesn't want to run into more danger.

"Although I only had a thin thread of hope as I watched the trophy deer run, fate appeared to be on my side. When the buck hit my trail, he put on brakes well within bow range. But I had a new problem to deal with, because the deer had stopped behind a fallen tree and offered no possibility for a shot. Then the buck leaned forward and exposed his neck.

"Even though the shot was at 20 yards, I knew I had to shoot instantly if I wanted to take it. I had bagged deer before with neck shots, and I also recognized that the buck might soon break and run. There are only a few seconds to shoot when a buck stops after smelling you. I knew the buck was aware I was there and that all his senses were attuned to danger. I quickly drew and shot. The broadhead cut the jugular vein of the buck, and he ran only 20 yards before he dropped.

"What made the hunt so memorable for me was the urgency of the shot. I had a trophy buck at 20 yards. I had to shoot quickly and accurately, and I had to be convinced immediately that I could and would make the shot. My body, my mind and my equipment had to shift from the world of premeditated action to instinctive action. All my practice with the bow, my knowledge of deer and my hunting experience had to weld together instantly. In less than six heartbeats, I accomplished my ultimate objective as a bowhunter."

INDEX

A

aerial photos   11, 110
anchor point   103, 129
angle of flight   42
arm guard   32
arrow   30, 41, 140
arrow rest   41
automatic aiming systems.   137

B

back wall   129
Bent Creek Lodge   82, 98, 117, 141
bleat call   73, 96
blood trail   46, 105, 131
body language   89
body odor   58
Boone and Crockett   55
bowstring   41
Bright Eyes   111
broadhead   30, 35, 41
broadside shot   45
Browning Company   144
brushing   144
Bushlan camo   80

C

camouflage   80
Carlton, Wayne   74
Caudle, Kathy   123
climbing tree stands   50
clothing   32, 41, 59, 63
Clough, Sherry   123
compound   27
cover-up scent   86

D

deer calls   66, 71
   See also bleat calls: grunt calls
deer sign   83
draw length   29

E

escape routes   18, 100

F

favorable wind   57, 111
Feather, Noel   41, 55
Ferguson, Byron   133
fletch   38
fletchings   64, 140
food tree   113
Forest Service   114
Foulkrod, Bob   63
funnel   22, 125

G

Game Tracker   64
Grace, John Demp   97, 107
Groom, Ronnie   113, 147
grunt call   61, 76, 79, 95, 96

H

Hale, David   76
Hart, Dave   124
High Country   123
Hill, Howard   25, 133
Hill, Jerry   133

I

inserts   36
Ishi   5

J

jump the string   43, 129

K

kill zone   127

L

ladder stands   51
Larson, Marlowe   144
let-off   29, 137
longbow   24, 133
lures   60, 66

M

man-drive   144
McIntyre, Ray   47
mechanical release   31, 103, 123, 130
Mossy Oak Full Foliage camo   84, 117

N

nock   39, 41
Norton, Larry   81

O

odor   113
overdraw   28

P

Pope and Young   5, 55
Pope, Dr. Saxon   5
Primos, Wil   71

Q

quartering shot   45
quiver   30

R

raingear   63
rattle   60, 77, 78, 79, 95, 96
recurve   25
run-and-gun   71, 73
rut   60, 77, 95, 98, 101, 127
Rutherford, Ellon   123

S

saddle   17
safety belt   47, 50, 51
safety video   54
Salter, Eddie   73
scents   60, 66

scrapes   18, 101, 127
Sheppard, Dr. Robert   35, 110, 141
shoot instinctively   134
sight   32, 41, 123, 130
Simmons, Jerry   11
spine   30
squat   92, 129
stabilizer   38
stalk hunting   81
string silencer   38

T

tab   31
target   32
Terrell, Regina   123
thermal   76
thermodynamics   76
thicket   18
throwing-the-call   74
topographical maps   11, 110, 114
trajectory   27, 28
tree stand   42, 47, 69, 71
   See also climbing: fixed: ladder; tree
      steps
tree step   49

U

U.S. Geological Survey   114

V

vanes   64, 140
video   73

W

Warner, Steve   78
Warren and Sweat Manufacturing
      Company   47
warring posture   95
Wellington Outdoors   117

Y

Yates, Clarence   23
Young, Art   5

Larsen's Outdoor Publishing
FISHING & HUNTING
RESOURCE DIRECTORY

If you are interested in more productive fishing, hunting and diving trips, this information is for you!

Learn how to be more successful on your next outdoor venture from these secrets, tips and tactics. Larsen's Outdoor Publishing offers informational-type books that focus on how and where to catch the most popular sport fish, hunt the most popular game or travel to productive or exciting destinations.

The perfect-bound, soft-cover books include numerous illustrative graphics, line drawings, maps and photographs. Many of our **LIBRARIES** are nationwide in scope. Others cover the Gulf and Atlantic coasts from Florida to Texas to Maryland and some foreign waters. One **SERIES** focuses on the top lakes, rivers and creeks in the nation's most visited largemouth bass fishing state.

All series appeal to outdoors readers of all skill levels. Their unique four-color cover design, interior layout, quality, information content and economical price makes these books your best source of knowledge. **Best of all, you will know how to be more successful in your outdoor endeavors!!**

HERE'S WHAT OUR READERS HAVE SAID!

"Larry, I'm ordering one book to give a friend for his birthday and your two new ones. I have all the BASS SERIES LIBRARY except one, otherwise I would have ordered an autographed set. I have followed your writings for years and consider them the best of the best!"
J. Vinson, Cataula, GA

"I am delighted with Frank Sargeant's Redfish Book. Please let me know when others in the Inshore Series will be available." **J.A'Hern, Columbia, S.C.**

**Great Tips and Tactics For
The Outdoorsmen of the Nineties!**

BASS SERIES LIBRARY
by Larry Larsen

(BSL1) FOLLOW THE FORAGE VOL. 1 - BASS/PREY RELATIONSHIP - Learn how to determine dominant forage in a body of water and you will consistently catch more and larger bass.

(BSL2) VOL. 2 BETTER BASS ANGLING TECHNIQUES - Learn why one lure or bait is more successful than others and how to use each lure under varying conditions.

(BSL3) BASS PRO STRATEGIES - Professional fishermen know how changes in pH, water level, temperature and color affect bass fishing, and they know how to adapt to weather and topographical variations. Learn from their experience. Your productivity will improve after spending a few hours with this compilation of techniques!

(BSL4) BASS LURES - TRICKS & TECHNIQUES - When bass become accustomed to the same artificials and presentations seen over and over again, they become harder to catch. You will learn how to modify your lures and rigs and how to develop new presentation and retrieve methods to spark the interest of largemouth!

(BSL5) SHALLOW WATER BASS - Bass spend 90% of their time in the shallows, and you spend the majority of the time fishing for them in waters less than 15 feet deep. Learn productive new tactics that you can apply in marshes, estuaries, reservoirs, lakes, creeks and small ponds, and you'll likely triple your results!

(BSL6) BASS FISHING FACTS - Learn why and how bass behave during pre- and post-spawn, how they utilize their senses when active and how they respond to their environment, and you'll increase your bass angling success! By applying this knowledge, your productivity will increase for largemouth as well as redeye, Suwannee, spotted and other bass species!

(BSL7) TROPHY BASS - If you're more interested in wrestling with one or two monster largemouth than with a "panful" of yearlings, then learn what techniques and locations will improve your chances. This book takes a look at geographical areas and waters that offer better opportunities to catch giant bass. You'll also learn proven lunker-bass-catching techniques for both man-made and natural bodies of water!

(BSL8) ANGLER'S GUIDE TO BASS PATTERNS - Catch bass every time out by learning how to develop a productive pattern quickly and effectively. "Bass Patterns" is a reference source for all anglers, regardless of where they live or their skill level. Learn how to choose the right lure, presentation and habitat under various weather and environmental conditions!

(BSL9) BASS GUIDE TIPS - Learn secret techniques known only in a certain region or state that often work in waters all around the country. It's this new approach that usually results in excellent bass angling success. Learn how to apply what the country's top guides know!

Nine Great Volumes To Help You Catch More and Larger Bass!

LARSEN ON BASS SERIES

(LB1) LARRY LARSEN ON BASS TACTICS is the ultimate "how-to" book that focuses on proven productive methods. It is dedicated to serious bass anglers - those who are truly interested in learning more about the sport and in catching more and larger bass each trip. **Hundreds of highlighted tips and drawings explain how you can catch more and larger bass in waters all around the country.** This reference source by America's best known bass fishing writer will be invaluable to both the avid novice and expert angler!

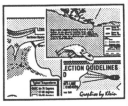

BASS WATERS SERIES
by Larry Larsen

Take the guessing game out of your next bass fishing trip. The most productive bass waters in each Florida region are described in this multi-volume series, including boat ramps, seasonal tactics, water characteristics and much more. Both popular and overlooked locations are detailed with numerous maps and photos. The author has lived and fished extensively in each region of the state over the past 25 years.

(BW1) GUIDE TO NORTH FLORIDA BASS WATERS - Covers from Orange Lake north and west. Includes Lakes Orange, Lochloosa, Talquin and Seminole, the St. Johns, Nassau, Suwannee and Apalachicola Rivers and many more of the region's best! You'll learn where bass bite in Keystone Lakes, Newnans Lake, St. Mary's River, Doctors Lake, Black Creek, Juniper Lake, Ortega River, Lake Jackson, Lake Miccosukee, Chipola River, Deer Point Lake, Blackwater River, Panhandle Mill Ponds and many more!

(BW2) GUIDE TO CENTRAL FLORIDA BASS WATERS - Covers from Tampa/Orlando to Palatka. Includes Lakes George, Rodman, Monroe, Tarpon and the Harris Chain, the St. Johns, Oklawaha and Withlacoochee Rivers and many others! You'll find the best spots to fish in the Ocala Forest, Crystal River, Hillsborough River, Conway Chain, Homosassa River, Lake Minneola, Lake Weir, Lake Hart, Spring Runs and many more!

(BW3) GUIDE TO SOUTH FLORIDA BASS WATERS - Covers from I-4 to the Everglades. Includes Lakes Tohopekaliga, Kissimmee, Okeechobee, Poinsett, Tenoroc and Blue Cypress, the Winter Haven Chain and many more! You'll learn where bass can be caught in Fellsmere Farm 13. Caloosahatchee River, Lake June-in-Winter, Lake Hatchineha, the Everglades, Lake Istokpoga, Peace River, Crooked Lake, Lake Osborne, St. Lucie Canal, lake Trafford, Shell Creek, Lake Marian, Myakka River, Lake Pierce, Webb Lake and many more!

> For more than 20 years, award-winning author Larry Larsen has studied and written about bass fishing. His angling adventures are extensive, from Canada to Honduras and from Cuba to Hawaii. He is Florida Editor for *Outdoor Life* and contributor to all major outdoor magazines.

OUTDOOR TRAVEL SERIES

by Larry Larsen and M. Timothy O'Keefe

Candid guides with inside information on the best charters, time of the year, and other important recommendations that can make your next fishing and/ or diving trip much more enjoyable.

(OT1) FISH & DIVE THE CARIBBEAN - Vol. 1 Northern Caribbean, including Cozumel, Cayman Islands, The Bahamas, Jamaica, Virgin Islands and other popular destinations.Required reading for fishing and diving enthusiasts who want to know the most cost-effective means to enjoy these Caribbean islands. You'll learn how to select the best destination and plan appropriately for your specific interests.

(OT3) FISH & DIVE FLORIDA & The Keys - Includes in-depth information on where and how to plan a vacation to America's most popular fishing and diving destination. Special features include artificial reef loran numbers; freshwater springs/caves; coral reefs/barrier islands; gulf stream/passes; inshore flats/channels; and back country estuaries.

(OT2) FISH & DIVE THE CARIBBEAN - Vol. 2 - _COMING SOON!_ Southern Caribbean, including Guadeloupe, Costa Rica, Venezuela, other destinations.

"Fish & Dive the Caribbean, Vol. 1" was one of four finalists in the Best Book Content Category of the National Association of Independent Publishers 1991 competition. Over 500 books were submitted by various U.S. publishers, including Simon & Schuster and Turner Publishing, Inc. Said the NAIP judges "An excellent source book with invaluable instructions for fishing or diving. Written by two nationally-known experts who, indeed, know what vacationing can be!"

DIVING SERIES

by M. Timothy O'Keefe

(DL1) DIVING TO ADVENTURE will inform and entertain novice and experienced divers alike with its in-depth discussion of how to get the most enjoyment from diving and snorkeling. Aimed at divers around the country, the book shows how to get started in underwater photography, how to use current to your advantage, how to avoid seasickness, how to dive safely after dark, and more. Special sections detail how to plan a dive vacation, including live-aboard diving.

M. Timothy O'Keefe was editor of the first major dive travel guidebook published in the U.S. The award-winning author writes for numerous diving, travel and sportfishing publications.

COASTAL FISHING GUIDES

(FG1) **FRANK SARGEANT'S SECRET SPOTS - Tampa Bay to Cedar Key** - A unique "where-to" book of detailed secret spots for Florida's finest saltwater fishing. This guide book describes little-known honeyholes and tells exactly how to fish them. Prime seasons, baits and lures, marinas and dozens of detailed maps of the prime spots are included. A comprehensive index helps the reader to further pinpoint productive areas and tactics.

(FG2) **FRANK SARGEANT'S SECRET SPOTS -Southwest Florida** *COMING SOON!!*

INSHORE SERIES

by Frank Sargeant

(IL1) **THE SNOOK BOOK-**"Must" reading for anyone who loves the pursuit of this unique sub-tropic species. Every aspect of how you can find and catch big snook is covered, in all seasons and all waters where snook are found.

(IL2) **THE REDFISH BOOK-**Packed with expertise from the nation's leading redfish anglers and guides, this book covers every aspect of finding and fooling giant reds. You'll learn secret techniques revealed for the first time. After reading this informative book, you'll catch more redfish on your next trip!

(IL3) **THE TARPON BOOK-**Find and catch the wily "silver king" along the Gulf Coast, north through the mid-Atlantic, and south along Central and South American coastlines. Numerous experts share their most productive techniques.

(IL4) **THE TROUT BOOK -**Jammed with tips from the nation's leading trout guides and light tackle anglers. For both the old salt and the rank amateur who pursue the spotted weakfish, or seatrout, throughout the coastal waters of the Gulf and Atlantic.

Frank Sargeant is a renown outdoor writer and expert on saltwater angler. He has traveled throughout the state and Central America in pursuit of all major inshore species. Sargeant is Outdoor Editor of the Tampa Tribune and a Senior Writer for *Southern Saltwater* **and** *Southern Outdoors* **magazines.**

HUNTING LIBRARY
by John E. Phillips

(DH1) MASTERS' SECRETS OF DEER HUNTING - Increase your deer hunting success significantly by learning from the masters of the sport. New information on tactics and strategies for bagging deer is included in this book, the most comprehensive of its kind.

(DH2) THE SCIENCE OF DEER HUNTING - Covers why, where and when a deer moves and deer behavior. Find the answers to many of the toughest deer hunting problems a sportsman ever encounters!

(TH1) MASTERS' SECRETS OF TURKEY HUNTING - Masters of the sport have solved some of the most difficult problems you will encounter while hunting wily longbeards with bows, blackpowder guns and shotguns. Learn the 10 deadly sins of turkey hunting and what to do if you commit them.

(DH3) MASTERS' SECRETS OF BOWHUNTING DEER - Learn the skills required to take more bucks with a bow, even during gun season. A must read for every man and woman who walks into the woods with a strong bow and a swift shaft.

FISHING LIBRARY

(CF1) MASTERS' SECRETS OF CRAPPIE FISHING by John E. Phillips - Learn how to make crappie start biting again once they have stopped, how to select the color of jig to catch the most and biggest crappie, how to find crappie when a cold front hits and how to catch them in 100-degree heat as well as through the ice. Unusual but productive crappie fishing techniques are included. **Whether you are a beginner or a seasoned crappie fisherman, this book will improve your catch!**

OUTDOOR ADVENTURE LIBRARY
by Vin T. Sparano, Editor-in-Chief, Outdoor Life

(OA1) HUNTING DANGEROUS GAME -It's a special challenge to hunt dangerous game - those dangerous animals that hunt back! Live the adventure of tracking a rogue elephant, surviving a grizzly attack, facing a charging Cape buffalo and driving an arrow into a giant brown bear at 20 feet. These classic tales will make you very nervous next time you're in the woods!

(OA2) GAME BIRDS & GUN DOGS - A unique collection of stories about hunters, their dogs and the upland game and waterfowl they hunt. These tales are about those remarkable shots and unexplainable misses. You will read about good gun dogs and heart-breaking dogs, but never about bad dogs, because there's no such animal.

LARSEN'S OUTDOOR PUBLISHING

CONVENIENT ORDER FORM

BASS SERIES LIBRARY ($11.95 ea.
or $79.95 for autographed set)
___ 1. Better Bass Angling Vol 1
___ 2. Better Bass Angling Vol 2
___ 3. Bass Pro Strategies
___ 4. Bass Lures Tricks/Techniques
___ 5. Shallow Water Bass
___ 6. Bass Fishing Facts
___ 7. Trophy Bass
___ 8. Bass Patterns
___ 9. Bass Guide Tips

INSHORE LIBRARY ($11.95 ea.
or $35.95 for autographed set)
___ IL1. The Snook Book
___ IL2. The Redfish Book
___ IL3. The Tarpon Book
___ IL4. The Trout Book

COASTAL FISHING GUIDES
($14.95)
___ FG1. Sargeant's Secret Spots -
Tampa Bay/Cedar Key

BASS WATERS SERIES ($14.95 ea.
or $37.95 autographed set)
___ BW1. Guide/North Fl. Bass Waters
___ BW2. Guide/Cntrl Fl. Bass Waters
___ BW3. Guide/South Fl. Bass Waters

LARSEN ON BASS SERIES ($14.95)
___ LB1. Larry Larsen on Bass Tactics

OUTDOOR TRAVEL SERIES
($13.95 ea.)
___ OT1. Fish & Dive The Caribbean
___ OT3. Fish & Dive Florida/ Keys

DIVING SERIES ($11.95)
___ DL1. Diving to Adventure

**HUNTING LIBRARIES/FISHING
LIBRARIES** ($11.95 ea.)
___ DH1. Mstrs' Secrets/ Deer Hunting
___ DH2. Science of Deer Hunting
___ DH3. Mstrs' Secrets/Bowhunting
___ TH1. Mstrs' Secrets/ Turkey Hunting
___ OA1. Hunting Dangerous Game!
___ OA2. Game Birds & Gun Dogs
___ CF1. Mstrs' Secrets /Crappie Fishing

BIG SAVINGS!
2-3 books, discount 10%
4 or more books, discount 20%

FOREIGN ORDERS
Please send check in U.S. funds
drawn on a U.S. bank and add $2
per book for airmail rate

ALL PRICES INCLUDE POSTAGE/HANDLING

No. of books _____ x $_____   each = $_____

No. of books _____ x $_____   each = $_____

No. of books _____ x $_____   each = $_____

 Multi-book Discount (%) $_____

TOTAL ENCLOSED (check or money order) $_____

NAME_____ADDRESS_____

CITY_____STATE_____ZIP_____

Send check or Money Order to: Larsen's Outdoor Publishing, Dept. RD93
2640 Elizabeth Place, Lakeland, FL 33813

We'll send this brochure free to a friend:
Friend's name_____Address_____
City_____State_____Zip_____

157

ADDITIONAL BOOKS FROM OUR FRIENDS AT...
NIGHT HAWK PUBLICATIONS
Please send me the following books:

_____ **DEER & FIXINGS COOKBOOK** by John & Denise Phillips
More than 50 years combined experience in preparing venison, a heart-smart meat with fewer calories and less fat and cholesterol but more protein than chicken, contains information on field and home care of venison as well as more than 100 proven venison recipes and more than 100 recipes for side dishes to accompany venison. **$14 each, includes postage and handling.**

_____ **OUTDOOR LIFE'S COMPLETE TURKEY HUNTING**
by John Phillips Includes the newest tactics from more than 35 of the best turkey hunters across the nation for hunting gobblers as well as more than 180 drawings and photos. **$27.95 each, includes postage and handling.**

_____ **FISH & FIXINGS COOKBOOK** by John & Denise Phillips
For all heart and health-conscious outdoorsmen, more than 125 delicious recipes for grilling, broiling, baking and frying saltwater and freshwater fish. More than 125 recipes for side dishes and numerous tips on handling fresh and frozen fish. **$14 each, includes postage and handling.**

_____ **TURKEY TACTICS** by John E. Phillips
Part of the North American Hunting Club's library, this comprehensive book covers the biology and habits of the wild turkey and gives a vast array of strategies for bagging them. **$21.00 each, includes postage and handling.**

_____ **DOUBLEDAY'S TURKEY HUNTER'S BIBLE**
by John E. Phillips
This widely researched book contains information for both novice and advanced turkey hunters on every facet of turkey hunting. **$14.50 each, includes postage and handling.**

Name_____
Address_____
City_____State_____Zip_____

Send check or money order to:
Night Hawk Publications
P.O. Drawer 375, Fairfield, AL 35064
Ph: (205) 786-3630; 786-4022
We accept Master Card or Visa
Call Toll Free 1-800-627-4295
Or Fax Credit Card order to (205) 781-0927
Please allow four weeks for delivery

ABOUT THE ARTIST

Sandy Hildreth, the artist of the painting, "The Hole In-The-Horn Buck" featured on the cover of this book as well as the illustrations in the book, is from Norwood, New York. A high school art teacher in a rural school in northern New York, Hildreth's days are filled with family activities with her husband and two children. Hildreth also enjoys doing illustration work and has numerous paintings and drawings for sale.

Hildreth, an avid bowhunter herself, has bagged whitetails, mule deer,

black bear, elk and antelope besides serving on the advisory staff of Precision Shooting Equipment for 10 years. She also has been a target archer with two national titles in the NFAA Bowhunter Freestyle Unlimited division and was both indoor and outdoor New York State Champion in the Open Freestyle Unlimited class.

According to Hildreth, she was so fascinated with the fact that a monster-sized buck with a magnificent rack like the Hole-in-the-Horn Buck had been found dead along railroad tracks in Ohio with what appeared to be a small bullet hole in one part of its antlers that she visualized how the buck would have looked alive with a bowhunter trying to take him.

"I imagined that deer jumping the string and bounding away to safety in another moment in my painting."

Contact Sandi Hildreth, 2 Crescent Drive, Norwood, NY 13668, (315) 353-2930 for further information on her outdoor paintings.

GARDENS OF MYSTIC SEAPORT
BOOK OF DAYS

THE MYSTIC SEAPORT MUSEUM®

JANUARY

1

2

3

4

5

6

7

Geranium
Buckingham House
Photo: Gene Myers

JANUARY

8

9

10

11

12

13

14

15

JANUARY

16

17

18

19

20

21

22

23

JANUARY

24

25

26

27

28

29

30

31

NOTES

January Gardening Tip:
Call the local Extension Service office to determine the last frost date
for your area; make up your seed-starting calendar and count back from the last
frost date to determine when each variety you plan to grow should be started.

FEBRUARY

1

2

3

4

5

6

7

Roses
Fence outside the G.W. Blunt White Library
Photo: Mary Anne Stets

FEBRUARY

8

9

10

11

12

13

14

FEBRUARY

15

16

17

18

19

20

21

FEBRUARY

22

23

24

25

26

27

28

29

NOTES

February Gardening Tips:
Call the local Extension Service office and order latest bulletin
on organic controls; inquire if gardening workshops are being offered.
Get lawnmower tuned up; clean up tools and equipment; have blades sharpened.

MARCH

1

2

3

4

5

6

7

Magnolia

Arch detail of the Thomas Greenman House

Photo: Mary Anne Stets

MARCH

8

9

10

11

12

13

14

15

MARCH

16

17

18

19

20

21

22

23

MARCH

24

25

26

27

28

29

30

31

NOTES

March Gardening Tips:
Most annual seeds need to be started this month; check your calendar.
Pull back mulch from bulb foliage starting to poke through
the ground; late frost will not hurt exposed foliage.

APRIL

1

2

3

4

5

6

7

Tulips
The North Boat Shed
Photo: Claire White-Peterson

APRIL

8

9

10

11

12

13

14

15

APRIL

16

17

18

19

20

21

22

23

APRIL

24

25

26

27

28

29

30

NOTES

April Gardening Tips:
Make lawn repairs this month as soon as soil is settled. Rake up winter debris
and apply slow release fertilizer. Fertilize shrubs, bulbs and perennial beds.
Apply oil for dormant scale before weather gets too warm.

MAY

1

2

3

4

5

6

7

'Ballerina' Roses
Wrought iron fence of the Bartram Building
Photo: Mary Anne Stets

MAY

8

9

10

11

12

13

14

15

MAY

16

17

18

19

20

21

22

23

MAY

24

25

26

27

28

29

30

31

NOTES

May Gardening Tips:
Divide perennials which need it now; share with a new
gardener in your neighborhood. Put stakes or chicken wire corsets in
for those perennials which will be flopping over by July.

JUNE

1

2

3

4

5

6

7

'General Jacqueminot' Roses
Trellis at Burrows House
Photo: Judy Beisler

JUNE

8

9

10

11

12

13

14

15

JUNE

16

17

18

19

20

21

22

23

JUNE

24

25

26

27

28

29

30

NOTES

June Gardening Tips:
Inspect for insect problems now, while they are most active. Hand picking is often
sufficient to control; aim for a least toxic approach. Get leaf mulch into flower beds before
plants get much larger; you will be rewarded in August for the effort made now.

JULY

1

2

3

4

5

6

7

Perennials and Annuals
River Garden with the New York Yacht Club in background
Photo: Judy Beisler

JULY

8

9

10

11

12

13

14

15

JULY

16

17

18

19

20

21

22

23

JULY

24

25

26

27

28

29

30

31

NOTES

July Gardening Tips:
Monitor rainfall now, and water deeply rather than frequently. Watering is best
done early in the morning before the sun is high. Side dress flower beds and vegetables
with fertilizer if needed, but not after this month. Replenish mulch where necessary.

AUGUST

1

2

3

4

5

6

7

Cone Flowers
Burrows House Garden
Photo: Judy Beisler

AUGUST

8

9

10

11

12

13

14

15

AUGUST

16

17

18

19

20

21

22

23

AUGUST

24

25

26

27

28

29

30

31

NOTES

August Gardening Tips:
Beat the heat; arise early to tend to garden chores. Enjoy the special
quality gardens have in the early hours. Deadhead annuals and perennials
regularly to keep them blooming. Stay ahead of weeds.

SEPTEMBER

1

2

3

4

5

6

7

Tiger Lillies
Burrows House Garden
Photo: Judy Beisler

SEPTEMBER

8

9

10

11

12

13

14

15

SEPTEMBER

16

17

18

19

20

21

22

23

SEPTEMBER

24

25

26

27

28

29

30

NOTES

September Gardening Tips:
Perennials can be divided this month. Continue watering if weather is dry.
Prune any shrubs which have bloomed since you pruned the spring-bloomers in June.
Prune and repot houseplants; bring them in the house before the weather starts to cool.

OCTOBER

1

2

3

4

5

6

7

'Angelique' Tulips
Memorial Garden
Photo: Katherine Cowles

OCTOBER

8

9

10

11

12

13

14

15

OCTOBER

16

17

18

19

20

21

22

23

OCTOBER

24

25

26

27

28

29

30

31

NOTES

October Gardening Tips:
Clean up garden as frost starts to take its toll; keep deadheading late
blooming plants. Install netting or wire to protect against winter foraging by deer.
Empty hoses and put them away. Bring garden notes up to date.

NOVEMBER

1

2

3

4

5

6

7

Ornamental Cabbages
Sailors' Reading Room
Photo: Judy Beisler

NOVEMBER

8

9

10

11

12

13

14

15

NOVEMBER

16

17

18

19

20

21

22

23

NOVEMBER

24

25

26

27

28

29

30

NOTES

November Gardening Tips:
Continue mowing lawn in areas mild enough to sustain growth.
Go through seed packets; store "keepers" in a plastic bag in the refrigerator.
Clean up garden tools and equipment. Paint and store outdoor furniture.

DECEMBER

1

2

3

4

5

6

7

Tulips and Daffodils
View overlooking Mystic village
Photo: Claire White-Peterson

DECEMBER

8

9

10

11

12

13

14

15

DECEMBER

16

17

18

19

20

21

22

23

DECEMBER

24

25

26

27

28

29

30

31

NOTES

December Gardening Tips:
Clean leaves out of gutters and give lawn a final raking. Add a layer of winter
mulch to perennials and roses. Prune evergreens judiciously for holiday decorations;
save extra branches to cover tender perennials after ground is frozen.

Your purchase supports the
maritime preservation work at Mystic Seaport